MW01639754

GURU AND DISCIPLE

By the same Author

Swāmī Parama Arubi Ānandam: Memoir of Fr J. Monchanin (out of print)

Saccidānanda: a Christian Approach to Advaitic Experience

Hindu-Christian Meeting Point—within the Cave of the Heart

The Mountain of the Lord: Pilgrimage to Gangotri

Prayer

In Spirit and Truth: an essay on Prayer and Life

The Church in India: an essay in Christian self-criticism

Towards the Renewal of the Indian Church

The Further Shore

The Secret of Arunachala: a Christian hermit on Shiva's holy mountain

ABHISHIKTĀNANDA

GURU AND DISCIPLE

An Encounter with Srī Gnānānanda, a contemporary spiritual master

I·S·P·C·K

GURU AND DISCIPLE : an Encounter with Srī Gnānānanda, a contemporary spiritual master. New edition, published by I.S.P.C.K., Post Box 1585, Kashmere Gate, Delhi 110 006, in 1990.

First Edition 1990
Reprinted 2000

Originally published in French as *Gnānānanda*, un maître spirituel du pays tamoul by Editions Présence (Chambéry) in 1970.
First published in English as *Guru and Disciple* "A Sage from the East" (translated by Heather Sandeman) by S.P.C.K., London in 1970.
In the preparation of this revised edition the help of Mr Maurice Salen is gratefully acknowledged.

Printed at Academy Press, E-40, Sector III, Noida.

Contents

Author's Preface		vii
1	Prelude	1
2	The Meeting	5
3	Tapovanam	17
4	The Brahmin Village	29
5	Alone in the Temple	38
6	The Shrine in the Jungle	47
7	Days of Grace	57
8	The One Essential	65
9	The Guru	82
10	Festivals at the Ashram	91
Glossary		102
Note		106

Contents

Author's Preface		vii
1	Prelude	1
2	The Meeting	5
3	Tapovanam	17
4	The Brahmin Village	29
5	Alone in the Temple	38
6	The Shrine in the Jungle	47
7	Days of Grace	57
8	The One Essential	65
9	The Guru	82
10	Festivals at the Ashram	91
Glossary		102
Note		106

Srī Gnānānanda

Preface

ONE of the best reasons for hope in the crisis through which at present the world is passing is certainly the growing interest shown by Western people in the East. Western man has in fact much to learn from the spiritual and cultural world of the East, which has evolved in ways very different from his own. Perhaps too it is only there that he will discover that inwardness which he so patently lacks and will recover that identity which seems to have escaped him—but this time an identity which will reveal to him the very depth of his own being.

This does not, however, mean that absolutely any contact with the East will enable the Westerner to have access to its true riches; and it would be even more untrue to suppose that this contact would act as a panacea which would cure all the evils from which present day society is suffering. Besides, East and West are complementary; both alike have much to learn from the other, in a great many different spheres. But this exchange will only be fully beneficial if it takes place at the right level—the only level at which it is possible to discover the East in its true character. At other levels an unbalanced exchange runs the risk of producing dangerous traumas on both sides. One only needs to think of the havoc caused by the sudden introduction of western techniques, however admirable they may be, in environments which are not ready for them. No exchange can be wholly beneficial unless it takes place in the context of a meeting of hearts at the deepest level of our being. Only at this depth, proper to each individual and yet in which all may mysteriously share, can those who come from different cultures and traditions truly meet and recognize each other; only here can each discover his most personal identity and at the same time accept the wonderful variety of individuals and cultures, thanks to which each finds in the other the possibility of his own growth and self-transcendence.

The sad thing is that when westerners come to ask the East for its secret, they too often set about it in the wrong way. Sometimes even today—

though this is becoming increasingly rare—westerners approach the East with the same pride and sense of racial and cultural superiority as marked the colonial period. That obviously makes impossible any true meeting of minds or exchange.

Even when the westerner comes to sit at the feet of the East with every appearance of humility and sincerity, this is still too often done with a mistakenly passive attitude. This causes him to expect, if not demand, an immediate answer to his problems, and not only that, but an answer which must fit into the framework of his own categories.

It is indeed this quest, wrongly understood and wrongly undertaken, that in these days launches so many people, young and not so young, 'on the road to Kathmandu', in search of the sages and gurus of Rishikesh, Benares and elsewhere. Alas, their quest seldom meets with success, and only too often ends in disappointment and frustration, with these unfortunate people then blaming India bitterly for not conforming with their preconceived ideas of it.

Most of these seekers, in fact, forget in the first place to empty the mind of all that is useless and irrelevant, and to open it up to its true depths—only there is it possible to hear the message of India. This message is diffused on every side in India, from its temples and holy places, and above all from truly spiritual people, of whom there is no lack, whatever people may say; but you have to know how to hear the message and how to recognize the true masters. The truth is that there are right and wrong forms of passivity. One kind is entirely open and receptive, all set to hear, like a perfectly tuned radio, free from 'interference', which at once picks up the waves from the transmitter. But there is another kind of passivity which is unfortunately more common; this refuses to make any attempt at assimilation and is not in the least concerned to rid the mind of its prejudices and preoccupations—but, if you do not take the trouble at least to open the shutters, how can you expect even the midday sun to penetrate into your room?

* * *

Some people, the intellectuals, ask India for *ideas*. Ever since Plato, and especially since Aristotle, the Mediterranean world has lived under the domination of the *eidos*, that is, of *thought* and *concepts*. It only knows things by means of the concepts which it has fashioned of them. But, as has been so clearly shown both by psycho-analysis and by modern structuralism, all concepts, however abstract, as well as the value-judgments which accompany them, are inevitably marked by the basic structures which underlie our thinking—our archetypes, our habits of speech, in short, our whole conditioning through heredity and environment—apart from which, of course, no one can live or grow humanly or spiritually.

India's grace is precisely that it makes us aware, at the deepest level, of this conditioning—those 'knots of the heart', as they are called in the Upanishads—by casting over the whole mental process the 'shadow', so to speak of the Unconditioned, which each of us bears at the very centre of his being.

Indian logic certainly has no cause to feel inferior to medieval scholasticism when it comes to splitting hairs, and the speculative discussions between different schools in India yield nothing to those of European theologians. However, as soon as one looks a little closer, one realizes that these discussions do not touch what is essential and that the conflict of ideas is always like the waves which play on the surface of the sea; underneath are the depths, supporting everything, beyond all discussion, beyond the reach of any words, unaffected by anything, and yet the foundation of all. In India the umbilical cord has never been cut, which links the experience of depth, one and unique, with the multiplicity of forms in which it is reflected at the various levels of the mind.

So long as westerners are intent on asking India for ideas, their expectations are bound to be disappointed. Of ideas India has enough and to spare, just like the West. For nearly three thousand years her philosophers have been examining the mystery of their inner experience in the light of Scripture and tradition. But these ideas, however different they may be from those of western philosophers, are all produced at the same mental level. They are never more than means of introduction to the mystery; and in that lies the whole secret of the guru's teaching. Conceptual structures can never either contain or enclose the *true*, as westerners too often tend to think. Whoever stops short at ideas, misses their message. The True can never be an object either to be possessed or to be made use of.

The real message of the East—Vedanta, Buddhism or the Tao—is on a different plane. It is vitally important that this should be realized, so that dialogue and communication may become possible between the very different cultural and spiritual worlds which coexist on this earth. But now the moment for this seems to have come, and this is one of the most valuable aspects of our *kairos*. Just as Christianity has existed for the last two thousand years within the closed world of Mediterranean culture, both shaping it and being shaped by it, so the cultural and spiritual world of the Far East has also developed in similar isolation. The moment has at last come, both for Christianity and for Eastern wisdom, to pass beyond their cultural frontiers, no longer simply in the persons of individual initiates or converts, but in a far fuller and deeper fashion. They will have to accept the fact that this universalizing, or catholicizing, process challenges the forms in which the original intuitions were expressed in the various particular and therefore limited cultures.

The real message of India, as we have just said, is concerned with setting mankind free from the 'knots of the heart', from that false identification which causes us to confuse with our real self one or other of the forms in which our personality manifests itself at the mental or social level. India's contribution to the world is first of all that it enables us to lay hold of the profound and ineffable mystery of our own being, the mystery of the 'unique and non-dual' Self, which even so is revealed in the multiplicity of conscious beings.

But once again, as soon as India says this, the westerner at once begins to speculate about what this Self is, about the meaning of the *Void*, the *nothingness*, the *fullness*, to which the Scriptures constantly refer. But then the *fullness* which is conceived is no longer *fullness*; nor does *nothingness* or the *void* have anything to do with what abstract thought seeks to lay hold of.

In the same way the Self that is thought about is no longer the Self; for if there is someone else thinking about it, what is left of its inalienable being?

When anyone has been struck by this experience, one can say that it is all up with him, at least as regards everything in which until then he had tried to express himself and realize himself. The 'I' of which he was normally aware seems to have disappeared. Now his 'I' is uttered at a depth of himself which no idea can reach and of which nothing can be predicated. His limited and introverted ego has been burnt up in this merciless flame. There no longer remains any room in him for a single atom of self-seeking or self-centredness.

For all that, the *jnānī* does not isolate himself from his fellow men, nor does he try to escape from his family or social duties on the pretext of guarding his inner solitude—though he may perhaps be plunged inescapably into the silence, as for example Ramana Maharshi was, just for so long as it takes for the mind to adjust to that overwhelming light. At the same time the *jnānī* will not immerse himself in works, *karma*, on the pretext of sharing his experience with his fellow men. Free and supremely indifferent, he will allow himself to be led by the Spirit, totally ready to go wherever he is taken.

Too often the westerner is attracted by what are mere substitutes for *bhakti* or *jnāna*. He is thrilled with pure abstractions or ideas about the supreme experience; or else he lets himself be taken in by 'experiences' which make him think he has attained to the heights. He thus lives in a pseudo-spiritual atmosphere in which his ego becomes vastly inflated without his realizing it, under the disguise of high-sounding talk about the *void* and *nothingness*. From the high ground of his aristocratic 'enlightenment' he harshly condemns those who still live at what he calls the lower level of myth and ritual, unmindful of the fact that he himself is living by a myth that is far more alienating than those which he decries in others.

Jnāna and *bhakti* are not any kind of particular 'mental states'; in their real depth they are experiences of totality. So long as only one side of human nature is affected—the intellect or the emotions, for example—we can be sure that the definitive experience is still remote. For India indeed spiritual experience is inseparable from the fundamental *conversion* which *mumukshutva*, the desire for salvation, necessarily brings about in the innermost centre of our being—that is to say, the integration of our being—through the choice of what has permanence, *nitya*, and the subordination of every activity of body or mind to the quest for this liberation, *moksha*. Moreover, the experience of the Self is precisely that salvation itself, which is the ultimate goal. This existential liberation has nothing to do with the purely intellectual knowledge of classical gnosticism or with the ritual initiation of the Greek mystery religions. It is a person's integration with his own depth, his coming to his own 'place of origin', as Ramana Maharshi used to say, completely free and completely open to the Spirit.

* * *

In the spiritual tradition of the West the closest equivalent to this experience of liberation is undoubtedly the *metanoia* or *conversion* which is basic to the message of the Gospel.

In both cases we are dealing with an experience of totality, an experience which meets a person in his awakening to himself, and beginning from this point of origin in the depth of his being extends to what seem to be the furthest limits of his personality. Evangelical conversion and Vedantin experience alike tear a person away from everything, within himself or outside, that keeps him in bondage. This indeed is that experience of the Spirit in which the Christian, once he is freed from his egocentric conditioning, is carried off inwardly to the Father, the primordial Source, and outwardly towards his fellow men; in this he discovers himself in his fullness through the unique, yet two-sided, transcendence of himself—with Jesus perfectly obedient to the Father, and prepared like Jesus, with Jesus, to give his life for others.

People have of course often tried to contrast Christianity with Indian wisdom on the grounds that the former is *karma*, good works, and the latter *jnāna*, contemplation. It so happened that one day Vinoba Bhave, addressing a group in Tamilnādu, advocated a combination of the wisdom, *jnāna*, of Vedānta, with the devotion, *bhakti*, of the Tamil mystics, and the good works, *karma*, of the Gospel. In fact, *jnāna*, *bhakti* and *karma* are paths, *mārga*, and should of necessity always be aiming at what is beyond them. Anyone who makes the road an end in itself, will never finish his journey. There are various paths to suit the variety of temperaments and vocations. But whoever takes pride in following the path of *jnāna* shows thereby that he is walking away from the goal. Moreover, no path is exclusive of the others, and progress on the path of *karma* is the touchstone of genuine progress on the paths of *bhakti* and *jnāna*—a point at which the profound wisdom of the Gospel path becomes clear. Besides, *jnāna, bhakti* and *karma* are only effective as paths when, at the level of thought, emotion or action, they are as it were reflections of the light which has already dawned in the depth of one's being. Their inspiration comes from beyond them; all of them belong to the realm of signs, and signs by their nature exist to lead beyond themselves.

If the fundamental Christian experience and the genuine Vedantin experience have so much in common, one may well ask why their respective formulations appear to be so different from each other, indeed to be quite incompatible—and that, even after making the greatest possible allowance for the mental and cultural contexts by which each of them is conditioned.

The problem is obviously not one that can be dealt with in a brief preface. However, it is at least possible to wonder if, posed in these terms, the problem is not a false one, arising once again from the assumption, inherited from the Greeks, that everything has to be solved on the speculative level.

In fact it is clear that, at the level of pure ideas, at the speculative level, no solution of the dilemma is possible. The experience of Jesus, which underlies all genuine Christian experience, is existential in character, just as is the experience of the Indian *jnānī*. Thought may indeed be able to glimpse something of this experience and to give a quiet hint to those who are alert and desirous of salvation, about how they may personally reach it and actually participate in it. But no concept could ever capture these experiences in any definition, still less transmit them. So, if both alike are inexpressible, what thought could compare them and pass judgment on them?

As a way of understanding this, one might perhaps refer to the ***ko'han*** of the Zen tradition, the paradoxes on which the novice is invited to meditate for months and years on end, until he comes to realize that there no solution, and in the very impossibility of solving it discovers the answer. But once again the solution does not lie in the logical conclusion that there is no solution; this would achieve nothing, except to burden the mind with a new idea, whereas what is at stake is precisely the getting free from all conditioning. All that happens is just that one day there is a break-through to the heart of things—but there is nothing that can be put into *words*. On that morning, when the disciple comes before his master, there is a light in his eyes; the master understands, and they both smile—and that is all...

The lofty rejection of Christianity in the name of a so-called higher Eastern wisdom is most often a proof of a total lack of genuine experience in either the Christian or the Vedantin context. Anyone who dares to judge and condemn has not yet discovered the depths. For the *jnānī* there can be no *ajnānī*. The only hard words that Jesus spoke were to the hypocrites and those who claimed to have all the answers!

The mind, naturally, protests because it likes to have the last word on everything. Pure water is without taste for the disputatious person who cannot resign himself simply to enjoy the flavour of absolute purity. He calls it taste-less, because he can only judge by comparison with what is spurious... 'He who has ears to hear, let him hear,' said Jesus. Let him who does not understand ask the Lord to open his ears, as the Psalm says (40:7). And may he open his heart within to the Spirit!

* * *

We would like to present the message of Sri Gnānānanda against the background of the above reflections. His message in fact seems particularly opportune at the present time, because it is so true and so clear.

The life of Sri Gnānānanda, just like that of Sri Ramana Maharshi, exhibits no trace of anything extraordinary.* No ecstasies, no siddhis, no esoteric teaching, no claim to have a mission, as is so often the case with so-called gurus; these corrupt their spiritual gifts which initially are often quite genuine, through an uncontrollable urge to dominate others and inflate their own ego. No more does Sri Gnānānanda put his disciples into

* When these paragraphs were written Sri Gnānānanda was still alive. He passed away in January 1974.

samādhi; he has nothing to do with any cut-price spirituality. The path which he teaches is basically one of total renunciation, whose final result is that no place is left for the ego to show itself. Anyone who doubts this should make trial of the path of *dhyāna* which he teaches!

He does not work through the medium of 'mental states' induced in his disciples as a means of helping them to enter into the mystery within. He goes straight for the essential, by a path which is as stark as that, for example, of the *Ascent of Mount Carmel*. In communicating with his disciples he makes no use of anything as a medium. His teaching goes directly to the very root of the master, to the source of the spirit. For sure, nothing of this can be felt, apart from that peace which shines out from him—and transforms those who can receive it.

His teaching is pure Vedānta. 'Vanya's' account of it makes no attempt to disguise the shocks or soften the paradoxes. It is in fact only these paradoxes which can get the better of our spiritual lethargy and can open up to the attentive reader levels of his being which are apparently new to him—but are precisely where the Spirit is awaiting him.

Anyone who has once discovered the dwelling-place of the Spirit in his own depth cannot be insensitive to the presence of this unique Spirit guiding everything in the world mightily and peacefully to its final consummation in Christ, the Omega point of the universe. Christians will then perhaps heed the call which this same Spirit, especially through the traditions and sages of India, is sending out to the whole world, and in the first place to the disciples of the Lord Jesus—a call that is always more interior, a call to the depths of the Heart of Jesus, to the bosom of the Father.

Gyansu, Pentecost 1970

1 Prelude

THAT morning Vanya had gone to the Ashram, as was his custom, for the singing of the Vedas.

He had sat down in his usual place in the Temple beside the wall among the group of devotees who came, morning and evening, to meditate near the *samādhi* of Sri Ramana, listening to the entrancing psalmody and helped by this rhythm to deepen their silent meditation.

The liturgy took its course. Seated in a group the children of the Vedic school sang the Upanishads, the *rudrapraśna* of the Yajurveda, Shankara's hymn to Shiva Dakshinamūrti, and finally the *Upadeśa Sāram*, a Sanskrit composition by Sri Ramana himself.

During this time a continuous procession was passing round the hallowed tomb. Each new arrival devoutly made the circuit, always keeping the monument on his right *(pradakshina)*, once, three times, or seven times. There were even some who made a vow to perform this ritual circuit one hundred and eight times each day. And every time that anyone passed in front of the *linga* which dominates the samādhi, he prostrated to the ground in worship and supplication.

Within the sanctuary the priests were busy with their own ritual, as little concerned with the singing of the children as with the movements of the devotees; for in worship as in life, each one has his own part to play, and the different roles do not interfere with each other. On the sacred stone of the linga the priests were continually pouring offerings of water, milk, clarified butter, coconut milk. After each libation they washed and dried the stone. In time with their litany of the one hundred and eight names of Shiva they offered it the petals of flowers. They adorned it with flower garlands and pieces of silk. They blessed and offered the *naivedyam*, the cakes of rice flour which would later be distributed as *prasāda*. Finally, amid clouds of incense they described circles in the air with flaming oil lamps.

At that precise moment the rhythm of the singing slowed down, the tone rose by a third, and everyone stood up, their hands joined together close to the chest. Then when the singers intoned the OM with which the Vedic recitation ends, all the joined hands were raised to face level and then above the head. Soon everyone was lying prostrate on the ground, in that highly symbolic gesture in which India expresses her inward experience of the divine transcendence and her total self-surrender to Him whose mystery she has recognized.

Meanwhile one of the priests had offered the final *āratī* with flaming camphor. He had murmured the customary mantras, but their sound was lost in the noise of the bell which he rang with his left hand, and even more in the boom of the temple gong reverberating under the granite vaults.

He then emerged from the sanctuary, carrying the brass plate on which the flame was burning itself out. Everyone gathered round and reverently stretched out his hands over the flame. Each one brought his palms, made holy by their contact with the fire, up to his eyes and then, taking a pinch of the sacred ash from the plate, applied it to his forehead.

Thus ended the morning worship. It always follows the same pattern, exactly as it was instituted in the days, now long past, when it was celebrated in the presence of the Maharshi. Vanya never failed to be present at it when he stayed at Tiruvannāmalai. Everything about it was for him deeply evocative—the place, the memories it recalled, the young brahmins with their long black locks, their white *dhotis* and their foreheads and bare chests marked with lines of ash—just like "Bhagavān" had been in his childhood, and indeed still was when he first came to Arunāchala. There was also the spell-binding effect of the rhythm and the language of the Vedas. Above all there was the presence—that of the Sage who had lived in this very place for so many long years, that of the mystery by which he had been dazzled and which had been so powerfully radiated by him. It was a presence which overarched and enfolded everything, and seemed to penetrate to the core of one's being, causing one to be recollected at the centre of the self, and drawing one irresistibly within.

* * *

After a final *anjali* towards the samādhi, Vanya turned and went out, paying more attention to his own thoughts and meditations than to the things and people surrounding him.

Suddenly a joyful 'Hullo' recalled him from his reverie. Harold came towards him, his arms outstretched and his face beaming as usual.

Vanya had already known Harold for some years. He had first met him in this very ashram one December evening when returning from one of his long walks on the mountain. That day, even more than usual, he had felt the overwhelming attraction of Arunāchala.

Long before this Harold had left his island home in the West and had wandered throughout the East in search of wisdom. In Ceylon he had sat at the feet of the disciples of the Buddha. In the Punjab he had questioned the Sufi masters concerning their secrets. For long months he had followed the pilgrim routes into the Himalayas. He had visited the holy places in North India, and also the great temples of the Dravidian country. For a time he had stayed in Pondicherry and it was there that he first heard tell of Sri Ramana's ashram at Tiruvannāmalai. People had insisted that he should at least visit this famous place which was so close, just a few hours by train or bus. They had particularly praised the pious and fashionable European community who lived there, devoted to the memory of the Maharshi. But Harold knew India too well to let himself be beguiled by the shrines or celebrities which draw the crowds.

One day however, when he was setting out for Cape Comorin he allowed himself to be persuaded to pass through Tiruvannāmalai and to stop there for a few hours—just to see the place. The few hours became a few days, the few days a few months, and finally two or three years passed without Harold having the slightest desire to move away even for one day from the holy mountain, Arunāchala. This year, for the first time, he had come away and gone in search of a little fresh sea air, for at that season the rocks on the mountain radiated an unbearable heat. He had now just returned from this short trip.

Vanya and his friend had hardly begun to exchange a few items of news, when Harold changed the subject and asked abruptly: 'Do you know the holy man of Tirukoyilur?' Vanya had to admit that he did not. In spite of his numerous visits to Tiruvannāmalai, he had never heard mention of any famous swāmī at Tirukoyilur, a little town which was hardly thirty kilometres from Tiruvannāmalai.

'He is a swāmī who is one hundred and twenty years old,' continued Harold. 'I myself knew nothing about him till last week. It was at Karikkal that I heard tell of him. A certain Govinda Pillai, one of his disciples, told me the most incredible stories about him. Each year he comes to Tirukoyilur to have his *darshana*. When he cannot come in person he at least sends him tributes in verse. He made me promise to pay him a visit on his behalf. Will you come with me?'

'Why not?' replied Vanya. 'After all, one does not meet centenarians every day. What is his name?'

'Gnānānanda; or I should say, Srī Swāmī Gnānānanda-jī Mahārāj!'

'Well, that's a fine name,' remarked Vanya. 'Tamilians seem to choose superb names for themselves. If only they always lived up to them! You know what Gnānānanda means? Simply "Wisdom and Joy" or, if you prefer, "The Bliss of knowledge". Did Govinda Pillai tell you exactly where he lives?'

'He wrote it down for me, to be on the safe side,' replied Harold, and showed his friend a bit of paper on which something like Kudameripatti was inscribed.

'I have never heard of that village,' said Vanya, 'but all we have to do is to go to Tirukoyilur and ask for directions. Anyway Tirukoyilur is a very interesting little town. For a long time I have wanted to go there. The trouble is that when I am at Tiruvannāmalai I can never make up my mind to leave it. You will do me a great service if you take me there. We can visit the three temples; the one of Vishnu-Perumal, and especially the two Shiva temples which are so bound up with memories of Ramana. You remember the story? The day he left home to answer the call of Arunāchala, he had not enough money to reach Tiruvannāmalai, but had to get off the train at Tirukoyilur. So he went to one of the temples where he received as alms a little of the rice offered during the worship. In another he spent the night and it was there, at the back of one of the little open shrines in the inner courtyard, that he had his famous vision of the Light, *Jyoti*, streaming forth from the summit of Arunāchala and calling him to "himself". '

2 The Meeting

TWO days later Harold and Vanya left Tiruvannamalai by the first bus. It was essential to leave early in order not to be overtaken by the heat of the day. In fact, they were chiefly looking forward to wandering round Tirukoyilur, but they must obviously first stop for a few minutes at the ashram of the holy man and make him an offering of fruit, as is the custom. They would also have to listen patiently to the exaggerated praises which his disciples would not fail to recount in his honour, as happens almost everywhere in the ashram world of India, and make at least a pretence of being interested in the spiritual platitudes that he would no doubt utter.... After all, Harold had promised Govinda Pillai that he would make this visit. He could not break his word.

As they climbed into the bus, Harold showed the driver the address which Govinda Pillai had given him.

'So you want to get off at the ashram,' the man replied, his face lighting up. 'Please don't worry. The bus passes right in front of it and I shall tell you when to get off.'

Harold and his friend were to learn later that in fact he was a disciple of Gnānānanda. Each evening, on his last run, he never failed to stop his bus in front of the ashram, taking just enough time to go in, prostrate, touch the holy feet, and receive the Swāmi's blessing. Regularly each evening he would also stop his bus somewhere in the jungle between Tirukoyilur and Tiruvannāmalai, in order to break a coconut under a sacred banyan tree and offer a few drops of pure water as a libation.

In later years when Vanya spoke of this expedition he used to say that, during the bus journey, the idea suddenly came to him that this day might mark a turning point in his life. But this seemed so very unlikely that he did not even give it a second thought. He much preferred peacefully to contemplate the sun which at that very moment was rising as a crimson ball, *aruna*, above the horizon and caressing with its first rays the slopes of the holy mountain, Arunāchala.

It was not yet seven o'clock when the two visitors reached Tapovanam—for that was the name of the ashram. This name was written in large letters on an arch over the entrance gate, as was also the name of the lord and master of the house; this had all been done at the request of his devoted disciples. In fact, the guru had only been living there for the last few months, and even then not continuously. The place where he usually stayed was ten kilometres further on, at Sittilingamadam, but the devotees from the town found that it was really too far away and too difficult to reach. Consequently one of them had given him this little house. So now people had only to cross the Pennar, which was a dry river bed for most of the year, in order to be with the guru and have his *darshana*. Sri Gnānānanda had allowed himself to be persuaded and had agreed, for the time being at least, to spend fairly long periods there.

Harold and Vanya entered the garden. There were only a few mango trees, a well, and in the middle, a characterless little house. None of the buildings which later invaded the compound were then in existence, nor was the temple which would one day stand in the centre—all of which would inevitably form a barrier between the grace of the guru and even the most fervent longings of those who would come from afar to see him. Our two friends had arrived just in time....

Vanya then noticed a young man who was returning from his morning ablutions. He went up to him and inquired about the Swāmi, apologizing for disturbing him at this early hour and offering to come back later if necessary.

'Please don't worry about that,' replied Krishnamūrti, 'Swamiji always makes himself available to anyone who comes to see him. Morning or evening, day or night, it makes little difference to him. In fact he scarcely sleeps all night. Just come along with me.'

Following Krishnamūrti they entered the house. The young Brahmin led them into the room on the right. At the back of the room, in one corner, the guru, Sri Gnānānanda, was sitting on a rickety old couch. He had short legs and his body was half enveloped in an orange dhoti, which left one shoulder bare, while one end was drawn over his head. He was unshaven. On his smooth forehead there was no trace of his hundred and twenty years!—only the three lines of ash worn by the devotees of Shiva and the vermilion mark in the centre. But from this deeply peaceful face shone eyes filled with immense tenderness.

The visitors greeted him with folded hands but did not prostrate nor even make the slightest show of touching the master's feet with their hands. Europeans always feel a certain distaste for these signs of respect, though in India they are perfectly normal and just as natural as genuflecting or kissing the hand in other places.

A carpet was brought and they both sat down. Vanya pushed his friend forward. After all, it was he who had a message for the Swāmi.

Harold began the conversation, speaking of Govinda Pillai and giving his greetings. He then went on to ask some questions concerning his 'doubts', to use the popular expression, about the spiritual life. Krishnamūrti translated Harold's questions into Tamil and the guru's replies into English. This quickly became extremely interesting. But the more interesting it became, the more the poor interpreter was out of his depth.

He was however a fervent and intelligent disciple. Each evening after his work he used to come to the guru and do everything he could to help him. He would spend the night at the ashram and the next morning would return across the Pennar to his office.*

There was no doubt about his having a good grasp of English, but the English required for the B.A. of Madras University is more suitable for science and commerce than for philosophy and mysticism! That day Krishnamūrti was clearly battling with subjects that were beyond him. Gnānānanda was well aware that the translation was not all it might have been and so kept on trying to give further explanations, but the result was only to entangle the poor interpreter in greater and greater difficulties.

Vanya soon joined in the conversation, first through the medium of English and then directly in Tamil. His Tamil was no doubt very elementary and his pronunciation lamentable. Yet soon there developed an inward understanding between him and the master which went beyond the words being uttered or heard.

---

* In the following year his faithfulness cost him his life.. The Pennar was in flood, but nevertheless he was determined to go across and set out on the causeway. Unfortunately the flood water submerged the road before he could reach the other side, and he was swept away by the current.

After a little while he asked,'What is Swāmi-ji's position concerning supreme reality? Is it *dvaita* or *advaita*? When all is said and done, does any difference remain between God and creatures? Is there at least some possibility for man to enjoy God and to realize this enjoyment in eternity?—or is there in the last resort nothing but Being itself, non-dual *(advaita)* and indivisible, in its infinite fulness?

'What is the use of such questions?' replied Sri Gnānānanda at once. 'The answer is within you. Seek it in the depths of your being. Devote yourself to *dhyāna*, meditation, beyond all forms, and the solution will be given you directly.'

The visitor went on to ask, 'Does Swami-ji perform rites of initiation?'

To Vanya's mind this was something of a test question. The eagerness of Hindus—and not only Hindus—for such practices, is well known. In the course of more or less elaborate ceremonies the disciple places himself under the guru's protection. The latter then secretly imparts to him some *mantra* which he will have to repeat faithfully, and sometimes adds some ritual that has to be performed. It is thought that the disciple is bound to make marvellous progress as a result of the almost 'magical' power of this 'sacrament', and to derive superlative benefits, both spiritual and material, from the recitation of the mantra and the performance of the ritual. And indeed the disciple's faith, if not the guru's grace, often does cause the initiation *(dīkshā)* that he has received to be effective. But very often also the swamis—for motives that vary greatly, as some only want to help their disciples, while others hope to extort a generous offering *(gurudakshina)*—show an anxiety to impart mantras which is only equalled by that of the devotees in asking for them. Even Sri Ramana's great disciple, Ganapati Sastri, regretted that his master would not agree to give mantras at least to beginners, and actually offered to do so in his place. For this reason Vanya awaited Gnānānanda's reply with special interest.

'Initiations—what is the use of them?' was again the reply. 'Either the disciple is not ready, in which case the so-called initiation is no more than empty words; or else the disciple is ready, and then neither words nor signs are needed. The initiation takes place of itself.'

He went on: 'So long as you perceive the world, it is ignorance, not-knowing, *a-jnāna*. When nothing of the world is any more perceived, it is wisdom, *jnāna*, the only true knowledge.'

The devotees now began to come in. Men, women and children, all made their prostration with reverence and love. It was easy to see that for them this was not an empty, conventional act, a formality required by good manners. Their bodily prostration was a clear sign of a far truer prostration which takes place in the secret place of the heart—showing their faith, their love, and their complete trust in this man who for them was nothing but the manifestation of the invisible Presence, the showing forth before their eyes of the grace and the love of the Lord himself, who dwells at once in the deepest centre of the heart and in the highest heavens.

The two Europeans, fearing that they might be in the way, asked permission to withdraw. They proposed to go to the town for a meal, visit the temples, and return later. The guru agreed, but would not allow them to depart without first seeing that they were given a glass of milk.

* * *

One hour, or maybe two, had passed since Vanya had sat down before the Swami, but he had scarcely noticed the time. He had not even felt the strain of sitting cross-legged, which normally troubled him greatly when he had to remain in this position for a long time without moving.

When he stood up again, everything seemed to have changed. He had come here out of curiosity, but found that the few words which this old man had said to him had gone home directly to his heart. There they seemed to have opened abysses of which till then he had no idea, to have released in his heart a spring of living water of incomparable sweetness. And yet all that had been said to him here was already familiar to him; he had read it, heard it, pondered it at length. He had learned nothing new at the level of words or ideas. But it was just that it had been repeated in such a way that a communication beyond words was established between the master and himself at the deepest level in each of them. All that the guru was saying to him seemed to Vanya to be welling up directly from the inmost recesses of his own heart.

In the course of his travels through India Vanya had met with those pedlars of wisdom whose disciples, Indian and European alike, vied with each other in boosting their guru's reputation. Here and there he had also come across some truly spiritual people, or at least some who were searching in complete sincerity for wisdom and realization. But now it seemed clear to him that he was in direct contact with the definitive experience of realization. And no one can have such a contact without paying the price. It is like a burn which marks you for life, whose scar can never be healed. It is a fire which never ceases to burn so long as there is anything left to be consumed, so long as this whole world, in its 'separateness' is not reduced to ashes.

As for this man whom he had approached almost as a tourist, Vanya felt that he had virtually taken possession of his very being. He realized that the allegiance which he had never in his life freely yielded to anyone, was now given without a second thought to Gnānānanda. He had often heard tell of gurus, of the unreasoning devotion of their disciples, of the way in which they surrender themselves totally to their guru—which to him, as a European with a mind shaped by Greek culture, seemed utterly senseless. Yet now, all of a sudden, that had become for him simple truth, plain fact, an experience that took him right out of himself. This man with short legs and unkempt beard, scantily clad in a loincloth, who had so suddenly burst into his life, could now ask him to do no matter what—even to set out like Sadashiva to wander on the roads, for ever naked and silent—and he, Vanya, would not even think of asking him for the slightest explanation.

And then, without even considering the matter, Vanya and Harold found themselves side by side on the floor, pressing the master's feet with fervent hands.

Vanya had had the darshana of the great Ramana during the year preceding his disappearance from this world. But in those days the Maharshi was only visible from the midst of the crowd and for the few moments allowed by the ashram authorities. Then too Sri Ramana was seated on the magnificent granite couch, like a throne, which had been carved to the order of his Bengali disciple Bose, in the main mandapa of the temple of the Mother...

Vanya had indeed gazed into those eyes which, like Gnānānanda's were so full of love and deep peace. He had sensed something of that call to the Within, which seemed to sound from the very depth of that man's awareness, now merged in the primordial mystery. It was surely that call which so often brought him back to the foot of the blessed mountain, to live in those same caves in which Sri Ramana had, as it were, been swallowed up by Arunāchala, the implacable. However, no words had been exchanged between the Sage and the man from beyond the seas. The Maharshi remained too *distant* for him to reach. He was separated from the crowd and from the enthusiasm of the devotees by the sanctuary with its oil lamps and dishes of incense, not to mention the privileged disciples who took turns to serve him and remained constantly at his side. At that time Vanya was still too fresh from Europe. He did not know the language, and above all he had not yet sufficiently penetrated the inner world to be capable of directly understanding the mysterious language of silence.

* * *

Beyond the experience of things and places, of watching or participating in worship, of reading or meditating on the Scriptures, of listening to lectures, there is the experience of meeting those in whose hearts the Invisible has been disclosed, and through whom the glory shines in all its brightness—which is the mystery of the *guru*.

The honourable title of 'guru' is unfortunately too often debased by being used inappropriately, if not sacrilegiously. No one should utter this word, let alone call someone his guru, if he himself does not yet have the heart and soul of a *disciple*.

It is in fact as unusual to meet a real disciple as it is to meet a real guru. Hindu tradition is right in saying that, when the disciple is ready, the guru automatically appears, and only those who are not yet worthy of it spend their time in running after gurus. Guru and disciple form a dyad, a pair, whose two components call for each other and belong together. No more than the two poles (of a magnet) can they exist without being related to each other. On the way towards unity they are a dyad. In the ultimate realization they are a non-dual reciprocity.

The guru is certainly not any kind of teacher; not a professor, nor a preacher, nor an ordinary spiritual guide or director of souls, one who has learnt from books or perhaps from someone else that which he in turn passes on to others. The guru is one who in the first place has himself attained to the Real, and who knows by personal experience the path that leads there; one who is capable of giving the disciple the essential introduction to this path, and causing the immediate and ineffable experience, which he himself has, to spring up directly from and in the disciple's heart—the lucid and transparent awareness that *he is*.

We may say that the mystery of the guru is actually the mystery of the spirit's own depth. To come face to face with the guru is to come face to face with the 'self' at that level of oneself that is at once real and most hidden.

The meeting with the guru is the essential meeting, the decisive turning point in a person's life. But it is a meeting that can only happen when once you have passed beyond the spheres of sense and intellect. Its place lies Beyond, in the 'fine point of the soul', as the mystics say.

In human encounters duality is still left intact. At their best we may say that a fusion takes place and that the two *become* one in love and desire; but in the meeting of guru and disciple there is not even a fusion, for we are in the sphere of the original non-duality. Advaita remains for ever incomprehensible to anyone who has not first lived it existentially in his meeting with the guru.

That which the guru says springs up from the very heart of the disciple. It is not someone else who is speaking to him. He is not receiving in his mind thoughts which have come from elsewhere and have been transmitted by sensible means. When the vibrations of the master's voice reach the disciple's ear and the master's eyes look deep into his own, then it is from within his own self, from the cave of his own heart, now at last discovered, that the thoughts proceed which reveal him to himself.

It therefore matters little what words the guru uses. Their whole power lies in the inward echoes which they cause. In seeing or hearing the guru, the disciple attains to the revelation of his own self, taking place at that deep level of himself for which everyone is essentially seeking, even if unconsciously.

The real guru is within us. Without the sound of words, he causes the attentive spirit to hear the 'Thou art that', *'tat-tvam-asi'*, of the Vedic rishis; and this real guru projects himself in some outward form or other at the very moment when his help is needed for taking the final step. It was in this sense that Ramana's guru was Arunāchala.

The only means of authentic spiritual communication is the *ātma-bhāsha,* the language of the ātman, the interior speech which is uttered in the silence from which the Word emerged, and which is only heard in the silence.

All of a sudden Vanya's mood changed. 'Now one can understand,' he reflected sadly, 'why the words spoken by the preachers who come from the West so rarely succeed in touching the heart of Hindus. And yet the Christ whom they proclaim is the supreme Guru. His voice resounds throughout the world for those who have ears to hear and, more truly still, he never ceases to reveal himself in the secret place of the heart. But when will their words and their life give convincing witness that they have not merely heard tell of this Guru, but that they have themselves met him in the deepest centre of their spirit?

'This meeting is what here we call *darshana,*' he said to himself. '*Darshana* literally means 'vision'. It is the coming face to face with the Real, appearing in a form that our human frailty can manage. There are the philosophical darshanas, the systems of thinkers which seek to approach the Real conceptually. There is the darshana of sacred places, *kshetra,* of temples, of holy images, *mūrti*, points where God, who transcends all forms, consents to appear under the manifold forms under which our human imagination, stimulated by faith, pictures him. Above all there is the darshana of the saints, which for those whose hearts are open is far more true.

'The darshana of the guru is the final step towards the ultimate darshana, in which the last veil is lifted and all duality transcended.

'That is the essential darshana which India has pursued since tho beginning—in which also India reveals her own secret and "in revealing herself to you, reveals to you your own most hidden depths".'

Long ago the rishis of the Upanishads had celebrated the mystery of the guru:

> Without learning it from another, how could anyone know That?
> But to hear it from just anyone is not enough,
> even if he repeats it a hundred, a thousand times...
> More subtle than the most subtle is that;
> it cannot be obtained by any discussion...
> Neither by reasoning, nor by ideas,
> nor even by the simple recitation of the Vedas,
> can it be known...
> Wonderful is he who can utter it,
> wonderful he who can hear it,
> wonderful he who knows it, having been well taught...
>
> *(Katha Upanishad, 2)*

> The brahmin who has examined the secret of the worlds
> that are reached by (performing) the Law and the Rites,
> loses all desire...
> Nothing transient can lead to the intransient...
> Renouncing the world and full of faith,
> he departs in search of the master
> who will reveal to him the secret of Brahman.
> With thoughts controlled and his heart at peace,
> he receives from him the ultimate knowledge,
> which reveals to him the True, the Imperishable,
> the Man *(purusha)* within;
>
> *(Mundaka Upanishad, 1.2)*

Nārada came before Sanatkumāra and said: 'Master, teach me.'

'First tell me what you know; then I shall know what to add.'

'I know the Vedas, the Puranas and all the sciences. I have mastered the mantras, *mantravid,* but I am not *ātmavid,* I do not know the ātman, I do not know *myself.* I have been told, sir, that those who came to know *themselves* were set free from sorrow. I suffer and am restless; help me to pass beyond sorrow.'

'All that you have so far learnt is only words.' Then Sanatkumāra led Nārada to know the mystery of the self, the infinite fullness which exists only in the self, and is itself present everywhere.

He made known to him the further shore, which lies beyond the darkness.

(*Chandogya Upanishad* 7.1, 24ff)

'All that I know, I have told you;
there is nothing beyond that.'
'Thanks be to you, Pippalada, thanks be to you!
You have enabled us to reach the further shore,
beyond ignorance.'

(*Prasna Upanishad* 6,7,8)*

* * *

Harold and Vanya left the ashram and set off for Tirukoyilur. There they visited the temples, beginning with the Vishnu temple, which is the largest and most famous.

The brahmins showed them round the temple, recounting the legends connected with it. The temple is dedicated to Vishnu Perumal in the form of his Dwarf-avatar, Vāmana; it recalls his being granted by Bali, the demon king who at that time was lord of the earth and even of heaven, as much ground as he could cover in three paces. The dwarf then, assuming a gigantic form, with one stride traversed the whole earth, with a second the nether regions, and with a third surmounted the highest heavens. The brahmins recited for them the verses of the Rig-Veda which celebrate this exploit of Vishnu:

He who strode across the three worlds,
who upholds the earth and the heavens,
he who with one step
attained the most exalted Light,
and there established for mankind
the final meeting place.

---

* The quotations from the Upanishads which are given in this book are freely rendered and do not aim at literal accuracy.

Vanya however never felt really at home in Vaishnavite temples. In them he sensed too much idolatry for his liking, as he often remarked. Those images and rituals seemed to him to issue from unfathomable depths of the subconscious, and he could not sufficiently identify with them to understand and enter into them.

On the other hand, the temples of Shiva always attracted him. The Puranic legends which later grew up around the person of Shiva could not conceal the very pure source in the depths of the Hindu spirit from which this myth originates. Shiva is above all the God who is Love, as they say in Tamilnādu. He is also the formless God, and the highest form of his worship is simply to disappear in him and to be no more capable even of giving him a name.

In the Shiva temple also the priests led their visitors round all the shrines, offering flowers, lights and incense in abundance. Harold made a longer pause in front of the image of Shiva Dakshinamūrti, to which he felt a special devotion. Vanya, on the other hand. lingered by the central shrine, where the silence, the stark simplicity and the darkness never failed to fascinate him.

Later on they sat down on a rock near the temple. Here someone came up to them and said: 'Just stand up and look over there!' Over in the north-west was the silhouette of Arunāchala, the holy mountain, which at that distance was reduced to the simple outline of its mysterious cone. 'This is where we come on the night of Kārttiki,' continued the brahmin, 'to have the darshana of the Flame'; and he made the Hindu sign of greeting. Vanya too joined his hands in an *anjali* to the mystery of that Rock, in the very place where the young Venkatarāma, in his flight from his father's home, had beheld the incorporeal Light... for Ramana, Gnānānanda, Arunāchala, every man and every being, and Vanya himself also, all mysteriously are murtis of the Formless One; to him all forms belong, and by allowing himself to be discerned under different forms, he little by little draws his chosen ones to himself beyond all forms.

3 Tapovanam

HAROLD and Vanya took their midday meal in the town, as they were afraid of causing trouble if they returned to the ashram at noon. They had realized that Sri Gnānānanda had in fact no servant or disciple living permanently with him. The disciples who arrived first each morning saw to the housework for him, and among them there was almost always some pious Brahmin woman who was delighted to prepare the master's meal. At other times food was brought to the Swāmi from the neighbouring *agraharam*. This was why our two friends returned to the ashram only in the afternoon; for as incorrigible Europeans they were terrified of upsetting others and, even more so, of being upset themselves. They then came to know, much to their regret, that the Swāmi had waited a long time for them that morning in order to have his meal with them.

Sri Gnānānanda was no longer in the little room where they had found him in the morning. He was now seated in the central room, which was scarcely big enough to hold the twenty or thirty people who squeezed in around him. As they came in, they prostrated, offered fruit and flowers, and then sat down facing the Swāmi, the men on the right, and the women on the left. Vanya had seldom had the opportunity of watching this ceremony from such close quarters.

If the devotee was a man, he came forward with the upper part of his body bare and a cloth knotted round his waist. He would begin by placing his offering at the Swami's feet, and then stepping a little way backwards, would join his hands in the anjali, prostrate himself flat on the ground with his arms above his head, and touch the floor with his forehead, each ear, and each shoulder. He would then raise himself on his knees or even stand up, put his hands together once more, and again prostrate himself full length, repeating the exercise three, five, or seven times, according to the fervour of his devotion. It is bad manners to prostrate only once and also a clear sign that one is not from a high caste. Finally the man would stand up for the last time, cover his ears with the palms of his hands bow low, touch the master's feet, and then touch his own eyes with the fingers that had been in contact with the body of his revered guru.

The women did not make a full prostration, but contented themselves with kneeling down and touching the floor with their foreheads. Sometimes a whole family entered together and out of courtesy the conversation would stop for as long as it took for father, mother and each of the children in turn to perform the rite.

When the time came to leave, the procedure was the same, but this time each person received a piece of fruit or a flower from the pile of offerings which had accumulated. This is known as *prasāda*, which the faithful receive with both hands and then reverently bring up to their eyes. Prasāda is in fact every grace which comes from above and also every sign of that grace. In particular, at the end of *pūjā* in the temple, it is the giving back to the faithful of what has been ritually offered. But prasāda is in a very special way the gift and sign of grace, when it is received from the hand of a saint or man of God, for they are more luminous manifestations of the infinite divine presence than other mortals. The guru's prasāda is always received with great devotion, whether it is a leaf, a petal, or a few crumbs of cake, and is then taken home to be shared with the family.

The children were quick to note that prasāda always accompanied the farewell prostration. As a result there were always some little imps who managed to make ritual entrances and departures practically continuously. The guru just smiled and always gave them something, so long as an orange or banana remained.

* * *

People used to come from the town and also from the nearby villages. Quite often they even came from Tiruvannāmalai, being former disciples of the Maharshi who were delighted to find a master once more whom their eyes could see, and to hear from his lips the very echo of Sri Ramana's teaching. Boys often dropped in at least for a moment on their way to and from school, especially those who lived in the nearby agraharam. On examination days not one of them would dare face the question papers without first being fortified with the Swami's blessing.

A poor woman came in, prostrated herself, and deposited her humble offering of fruit and flowers. As usual the Swāmi held out his arms in a gesture, or *mudra*, of grace and murmured, 'Om Deva.'

'Well, ammā, where do you come from? Is all well in the village? at home? How are your husband and children?'

The woman began her long story. Her village was at least thirty kilometres away. She and her elder daughter had already been to see the Swāmi, but that was in the other ashram at Sittilingamadam. The Swāmi had then blessed them both, and his blessing had borne fruit. This time she had come on her own, but it was again anxiety about her daughter that had brought her. The girl was of marriageable age and there ware two cousins who were asking for her hand. According to the customs of their caste, the cousins were both equally eligible. The poor mother was distraught, wondering which of the two she should choose for her daughter. In desperation she had come to ask the guru's advice.

The village woman explained everything rather laboriously, and her dialect was not easy to grasp. When people had finally understood, there was a great burst of laughter. The Swāmi was the only one to keep a straight face. He asked very gently for details, inquired what the girl felt about it, asked more questions about the boys, and then suggested to the woman that she sit down quietly. After a little while, he spoke to her again, encouraging her and telling her to come back the next month after the fast of the full moon, and to bring her daughter with her.

After that two peasants appeared at the back of the room, looking apprehensive and ill at ease. They remained near the door, leaning against the wall, not daring to come forward, far less prostrate. However Sri Gnānānanda had noticed them. He asked them what was the matter and what they wanted. The poor peasants mumbled their request, and the Swāmi's reply rang out clearly:

'If you are ill, go and see a doctor who will give you all the pills and medicines you require. If your wife or daughter is in the grip of fear or being harassed by evil spirits, go to an exorcist. Very near here there is a Muslim who is a past master in the art of driving out evil spirits. If it is for spiritual ignorance that you are seeking a cure, then come here. But be very sure that here we have no medical doctor or exorcist. We deal only with spiritual sickness.'

One of the visitors asked Sri Gnānānanda to explain the name of the ashram, *Tapovanam*, which he did as follows:

'*Tapas* means intense heat, and so, fervour, austerity, ascetic practice. *Vana* (in Tamil, *vanam*) means a wood or forest. In old days there were in India vast forests and jungles, where hermits could withdraw far from human society, living off wild fruit and roots, and passing their time in contemplating the things of God. But at least in this part of the country there are hardly any forests left. They have all been cut down, transformed. Therefore, if we no longer have a forest, we must at least set apart certain places where those who have the desire may go and lead without disturbance a life of asceticism and prayer. This ashram has been founded specifically for those who want to devote even a small part of their time to spiritual pursuits, far from crowds and their habitual worries. Here they can receive suitable teaching and apply themselves to meditation.'

The talk continued. Starting from the most commonplace matters, the guru always found ways of raising the mind of his hearers towards the things that really matter and to the only real problems. In every case he showed an inexhaustible kindness.

Vanya was sitting close to him, eagerly drinking in all that he said. He soon noticed that the Swāmi was making quiet but repeated enquiries whether the milk had arrived, and realized that this was on account of himself and his companion. As the guru had not been able to offer them a meal at midday, he wanted to provide them at least with some refreshment before they left.

Then Vanya spoke up : 'Swamiji, why do you worry about it? It was not to get food for our bodies that we came here. Our thirst is for the milk of wisdom. Please teach us. Truly we need nothing else.'

Speaking very gently, and scarcely opening his lips, the Swāmi replied quietly and deliberately:

'There is a time for spiritual and a time for bodily food. The little calf cannot always have his mother's milk when he wants it. She knows when to give it to him, and how much to allow him. It is the same with the milk of knowledge.'

Whether the time was right or not, in any case all who were present did their best to make the most of the spiritual banquet, and asked the Master every possible question about *jnāna*, wisdom, and *dhyāna*, the path that leads to it.

Unfortunately, sitting beside the Swāmi was a visting sādhu, Shivaprākasham by name, which means 'the glory of Shiva'. He did not know either English or Tamil very well, as he came from the Kannada country where he was said to have been a journalist before he took *sannyāsa*. Nevertheless he was continually interrupting, sometimes even before the guru had a chance to answer a question, and making comments on what the guru said. At times his toothless mouth was wide open, at others his face was contorted in a self-satisfied smirk, while he made pompous gesticulations and always spoke at the top of his voice.

Vanya was greatly irritated, and soon realized that others shared his feeling. So he said to the bore: 'Mahārāj, we came here to profit from Guruji's teaching, which he imparts to us in his own inimitable fashion. Commentaries only spoil the effect of his words. He alone is the one we want to hear and to hear him in silence ..'

The Kanarese sādhu took him up at once: 'Silence is this; silence is that', quoting śloka after śloka in praise of silence. Vanya with difficulty restrained himself from telling him point blank that in the first place silence means keeping your mouth shut!

Quite unconcerned, Shivaprakāsham continued to talk. He demanded the names of the two westerners, where and when they were born, and all sorts of other details. That morning the guru had quietly asked them a few questions, less from curiosity than out of courtesy, and in order to be able to introduce them to others. It was enough for him to know that his two visitors were originally from Europe, that they had come to India some years earlier, and were living in such and such a place, devoting most of their time to meditation and silent prayer. He was not interested in their names, nationality, religion, and the rest.

Vanya then said to the tactless sādhu: 'I am sorry, Mahārāj, but especially between sadhus such questions should not be asked. They have no meaning. As soon as anyone has received sannyāsa, he ceases to have a country or home of his own. His address is simply the place in which he happens to be at the moment. As for his country, his birthplace, where he is coming from and where he is going—if you insist on speaking in these terms—are they not simply that "cave of the heart" of which the Scriptures speak, and into which he is always seeking to enter more deeply? This ochre robe which I am wearing is precisely the sign that on the day when I took it, I renounced everything, and that I no longer have the right to say that anything whatever on earth is "mine". What I was or where I was, yesterday or ten years ago, is utterly irrelevant. What does it matter where this body was born, or what name it was given by those who first held it in their arms? The sadhu no longer possesses either name or country—indeed, he is not supposed to possess even an " I ".'

Swāmi Gnānānanda was visibly pleased by Vanya's reply. Looking at him, but addressing Shivaprakāsham, he said quietly: 'Why ask him such questions? He should not even be able to remember the things you are asking about.'

Milk and coffee, accompanied by fruit and cakes, were now brought in. Vanya and Harold were taken into the adjoining room, so that they could enjoy them in peace. The mail also arrived at this point, and everyone went off here and there in the house or the garden. The Swāmi, still very agile despite his hundred-and-twenty years, sat cross-legged on the low wall of the verandah and had someone read out the cards and letters which had just come. Anyone was free to listen—for, after all, there was nothing private in them. In fact their contents were almost always the same. People wrote to thank Swamiji for his blessing, for the favours obtained through his prayers, his always kindly hospitality. Even more frequently they told him about problems over money or health, asked for his blessing, sought his prayers for their children's studies or for forthcoming marriages. When he had heard them all, Gnānānanda proceeded to dictate replies, giving to each one at least a word of encouragement, promising to remember him and giving his blessing.

* * *

Behind the house there was a large mango tree, and close to it a huge tree stump. Vanya went and sat down on it, away from the crowd.

However, he had not been there for more than five minutes when a group of brahmins approached— not without first having asked the guru's permission, as he dscovered later. He protested vigorously when he saw them preparing to make their ritual prostrations in front of him. 'How can you do such a thing in the ashram of such a unique Swāmi?' he asked; 'any sign of respect should be paid only to him.'

The only result of this little homily was to make them even more convinced that he was a saint. They then sat down round him and began to converse, half in English and half in Tamil.

Some of them were from Tirukoyilur, and others from the neighbouring agraharam. Among them was the lawyer who had donated the house and property to Sri Gnānānanda. Another was a police officer, and others were farmers. As a result of Vanya's reply to the indiscreet questions of Shivaprakāsham, they had no desire to seem over-curious in his regard. Besides, as so often happens in the Hindu world, answers on the spiritual level to questions asked about worldly matters give no less satisfaction to the questioner. Indeed, when people have the darshana of a sannyasi they look to him above all for help and inspiration to rise above their daily preoccupations and to draw near to the mystery of the heart, which always so fascinates the truly spiritual Hindu. The conversation in fact mainly revolved round the Swami, for whom they all showed boundless veneration.

' When I was a young man,' one of them reminisced, 'I respected neither faith nor law and was the despair of my parents. In particular I despised sadhus, those idlers... but now in spite of my education, my status and financial position, I know no greater joy or honour than that of prostrating before them, having their darshana and serving them. Not a day passes without my coming here with my wife and children at least for a few minutes in order to receive Sri Gnānānanda's blessing. This transformation is due entirely to him. Through him I have once more found God.'

'His blessing is always with us,' continued another, 'and we have often had solid proofs of it. One day my child was at the point of death. I had often entreated Swamiji on his behalf, but his illness had continued and grew worse. On that day we had lost all hope, and it was just a question of hours. I was at the end of my tether, but got into my car and rushed over to Swamiji. At least he would give me a little strength to bear my trial. When I got there, I prostrated, and between sobs told him about my son's condition. He lifted me up and fixed his eyes upon me—those eyes filled with compassion which you also have now seen. "Your child?" he said: "why are you so anxious ? He is perfectly well now." I refused to believe him, but he insisted that it was so, and told me to return home at once. When I reached home my child was out of danger.'

The personal history of the Swami, however, remained for everyone shrouded in mystery. What was certain was that he had come to Sittilingamadam about thirty years before. At first he had lived in the temple, observing silence and begging for his food. At that time he had immensely long hair which reached down to his feet, though on occasion he used to wind it round his head. His only clothing was the *kaumanam*, a small strip of cloth between his legs. After some time he was persuaded to stay in some outhouses, and then he was presented with a house. After that he no longer needed to beg for his rice, as there was always someone to look after his needs. He ceased to observe silence and began answering the questions that people asked. One day he cut off his long hair and put on a dhoti. His reputation spread throughout the district, and people came even long distances to see him, ask his advice and receive his blessing.

And before that? Before that he had been near Salem. A large ashram had been built for him there, which was now empty. He went there occasionally in order to please his disciples in that area, who were mostly poor weavers. People said that he had spent twenty or thirty years there.It was also said that before going to Vellanatham he had lived in the Coimbatore district at a place called Vannandur. There were other ashrams, too, which bore his name, at Krishnapuri, Bhavani, Idappadi, Anangur. It seems that he would arrive in a certain place and settle down there to meditate. Gradually his reputation would grow and an ashram would be built for him. He would then remain for some time, teaching anyone who would listen, and then one fine day he would disappear. At Vellanatham ashram, near Salem, there is supposed to be a calendar for the year 1872. The Brahmin who gave this information then summed up: 'As long as the Swami is willing to live amongst us, let us make the most of it and try not to do anything that might displease him and make him go off somewhere else.'

Sri Gnānānanda himself was always very reserved when speaking of his former life. When someone asked for exact information, he invariably replied that he would give it to him later. When someone wanted an exact date, he would say 'Oh that happened a long time ago, a very long time ago!' However his place of birth was known or thought to be known—Mangalagiri in the Kannada country. His father was Venkatapati Rao, his mother Chandasikla Bai. He ran away from home at the age of eleven or twelve, after a quarrel with his elder brother who had beaten him. He then met a sadhu and accompanied him to the Himalayas. But others said that he came first to Vellanatham and went to Kashmir from there. There is no doubt that the visit to Kashmir marked a very important stage in his life; he never referred to it without a certain nostalgia, though he never gave any details of what had taken place there. After that he travelled all over India, and also Ceylon and Burma, as sadhus often used to do during the days of the British Empire. One day he confided to Vanya that he had met Sai Baba, the Maharastrian Saint. In addition to all this he had a very detailed knowledge of places in Tamilnādu.

It was apparently only after about forty years of wandering or solitary ascetic life that he officially took sannyāsa. As he had given the name of the guru who initiated him, his *vamsha,* or genealogy as a sannyāsī, could be drawn up from guru to guru. His disciples had had it printed, and it can be seen in a frame which hangs in the darshan hall beside the Tamil and Sanskrit tributes, which people sent to him on his birthday.

Then what about his age? Many people said that he was a hundred and twenty years old. Others, calculating by astrology, have made him out to be a hundred and fifty-three. But how could he possibly be so old? He was still so agile, walked so briskly, and himself drew the water from the well for his morning bath. He also enjoyed excellent health, directed every smallest detail in the life of the ashram and supervised all the new building projects. On his face there was no sign of a wrinkle. Certainly, anyone looking at him would find it difficult to believe that he had reached seventy.

But then, is it possible to find room for such a long series of events in such a short space of time? The only possibility—one which in fact later investigations tended to support—is that, in an unconscious desire to magnify the guru, his sojourns in different places have been regarded as following each other in succession, when in fact they were dovetailed together during the same period of time.

Someone in the group produced a leaflet printed in Tamil. This stated that Sri Gnānānanda appeared in this world on 30 January 1814! Its author was a woman disciple who lived in Bangalore. The Swāmi himself had told her everything and had actually dictated his life history to her one day when she was deep in meditation in her private prayer-room. To be precise, it was Sri Murugan—the God-Child, the Beautiful God, of the ancient Tamil tradition—who appeared to her; and in her mind there was not a shadow of doubt that Gnānānanda was truly the *avatāra* of Sri Murugan, who thus apppeared in human form to comfort and save his devotees. One day, when someone faced this fervent disciple with certain historical facts and dates which could not be squared with her account, she replied with total conviction that her sources were superior to any human document.

Murugan Das then spoke: 'The guru is at least two hundred years old. I have heard him say that one day he was seated in *samādhi* near his hermitage at Anangur in the forest of Perambalur, when prince Navalu came there to hunt deer; but on catching sight of him, the prince was terror-struck and fled. How could that have happened, if he was only born in the last century?'

He also said: 'Guruji was already here beside the Pennar river when the young Ramana, who had also run away from his home, got down at Akhanandanallur and spent the night in the temple. It was he who fed him and sent him on to Tiruvannāmalai'.

'He also knew Auveyar, the poetess of the Sangham, the sister of Tiruvalluvar.' But Auveyar lived twenty centuries ago!

However, in all this, on what level are we operating? When a jnānī speaks to us, do we ever know the level from which he is speaking? No more than the prophet's vision of the future, can the sage's view of the past be pinned down to the chronology which measures the world of external events. He may be speaking at the level of the ātman, which alone is real; or again, he may be using the language of ordinary experience, so that his words may be within the grasp of his hearers. The atman is not-born, it is everywhere, transcending time and space.

This particular form which we call the body of such and such a jnānī, does not seem to him to be any more *his own* than all the other forms, human or whatever, in the created world. The very term *jnānī* itself is misleading, because by definition it implies particularization, and therefore a distinction between the jnānī and the so-called ajnānī— and that, in the light of the ātman, makes no sense.

In truth, the one who has realized the ātman is in every place and every time. He is the young Ramana running away to Arunāchala, and he is the priest who gave him food on his way. He is the hermit meditating in the forest in the time of the rajahs, and he is the sannyāsī who met Auveyar. He is Yājnavalkya who revealed to king Janaka the upanishad of being, and he is the rishi who in the first age heard the Vedas. Indeed, he is Shiva himself, seated under the banyan in the jungle, wearing his tiger skin and with his third eye annihilating Kāma, Love the Tempter, who sought to divert his attention— Shiva who on another day, as Dakshinamūrti, taught through his silence the four sons of Brahma in their ignorance of the highest wisdom. He is the Formless, the Not-Born, who in every form reveals something of himself and in every birth appears afresh.

Vanya then said: 'What does it matter to us to know if Swamiji is fifty, two hundred, or even four hundred years old? Will knowing that give us *moksha*, salvation, the vision of the One who Is? What use is it to us to know what he was yesterday or what he will be tomorrow, to know where he was sixty years ago, or where he will be in a hundred years' time? Even when he speaks to us in human terms, apppearing to us as he does at this time and on this day, for us he is first and foremost the one through whom we receive the word of liberation, the Lord's summons to what is within. Surely the essential thing for us are the words that he speaks to us and his look which penetrates our hearts? And as for the obscurity which he allows to veil everything that does not belong to the present moment, that after all seems to be his way of impressing upon us his supreme lesson, which is that the only moment that matters is that in which we become "aware of our self".'

* * *

The sound of chanting now became audible. It came from some brahmins who were beginning to recite the *Vishnu-sahasra-nāma*, the litany of the thousand names of Vishnu, as was done every afternoon in the darshana room. This indicated that the guru was once again in the house, and soon everyone was seated round him.

When the chanting was ended, Vanya went up and said: 'Swamiji, I came this morning more or less out of curiosity, and see what has happened! For years I have been coming to Tiruvannāmalai and staying there for months on end, so close to you; but until this week I had not even heard your name. How was it that all this should come to pass only today?'

Gnānānanda's reply was very simple: 'It happened because the right time and the right moment for you had come.' And he added:

'Come back here and stay with me. We shall resume our talk. Above all you will be free to devote yourself to silent meditation. No one will disturb you. You will not need to worry about food or anything else. Apart from our conversations, you will be left in silence. So come back after a few months, after the festival of Pongal. I shall be expecting you.'

4 The Brahmin Village

NEXT year, at the beginning of spring, as had been agreed, Vanya returned to Tapovanam, this time alone.

Sri Gnānānanda had arranged to meet him on that Sunday. He himself had to return to Tirukoyilur on that day, after a short visit to his hermitage at Sittilingamadam. So Vanya arrived at the ashram during the afternoon. A young man from the neighbouring village of Kusipalayam was busy watering the flowers and young trees. Recognizing Vanya, he said: 'Swamiji will only get back tomorrow morning. In the mean time, make yourself at home in the room he has kept for you.'

Vanya had brought some fruit with him to make the customary offering to the Swami. This would do for his supper, as by the next day it would have gone off. Besides, what is once offered in intention can surely be regarded as prasāda.

Monday morning passed without a sign of Sri Gnānānanda, and in fact not a soul came near the ashram.

Vanya discovered later how impossible it was for anyone to anticipate the Swami's movements. The decisions of a jnānī are seldom complicated by lengthy consideration; besides, how could he ever feel himself in any way bound? He acts on the inspiration of the moment. Who can ever tell whence he will come or whither he will go at the prompting of the spirit in him? It sometimes happened, for example, that Sri Gnānānanda would make all the arrangements for some journey. At the appointed hour a devotee would arrive from the town in his car, having dropped everything, to take the Swami where he wanted to go. But if the guru happened to be busy, for instance, with some visitor who had just unexpectedly arrived, he would postpone his departure until the following day. The disciple would silently prostrate and take his leave. Hardly would he have reached home, when an express messenger would arrive to recall him. Without saying a word or even trying to find some justification or explanation, the disciple would immediately return and pick up his revered master.

'He knows better than we do what is best for us,' concluded the brahmin who was telling Vanya the story a few days later. 'We should realize how incredibly fortunate we are, that he accepts our humble service.'

Midday came. No sign of the guru, or of anyone coming to the ashram. Vanya began to feel hungry. Tirukoyilur was really too far off by the main road, and at that time of day it was impossible to take the short cut across the river, as the sand would be blazing hot. 'A golden opportunity to live like a real sadhu at least for one day,' he thought; 'I can go out and get my food by *bhikshā*.' He had in fact, a few years earlier, made one attempt to do this. On that day he had first gone to meditate in the underground crypt of the Pātāla Linga inside the great temple at Tiruvannāmalai, the every place where Ramana Maharshi had stayed for a long time in his youth. Then, on the advice of Arunachala Ayyar, an old brahmin who had once been the Maharshi's companion on the mountain and now lived in the temple, he had traversed the three streets where he felt sure that in almost every house someone would gladly give him alms in the form of a little rice. But alas, his courage failed him, and he had not dared to approach a single door... This time, however, he felt more confident. Also in the agraharam to which he was proposing to go, there were many people whom he had met on his first visit to Tapovanam. They would surely fill his bowl! So Vanya took up his staff and begging bowl, wound a towel round his head, for the midday sun was at its hottest, and resolutely set out for the village.

As he went along, he asked people to show him the way to the agraharam, or Agaram, as it was called locally. This led to various brief conversations with the country folk whom he met on the way. One of these had accompanied him for a while, and when he had to leave him, because his path led off to one side, he said,

'Swāmi, will you kindly stand here for a moment?'

'Why?'

'So that I can make my *namaskāram* to you, of course!' And without waiting for permission, he prostrated himself on the ground. For a believing Hindu it is a blessing to meet with a sannyāsī. When he prostrates before him, he is paying homage to the Master of the universe and the Lord of the secret place of the heart. Whereas a European's only thought would probably have been to take a photo of the strange man! Truly we have much to learn from those whose hearts are humble and simple—those for whom Jesus gave thanks to his Father.

Vanya soon reached the agraharam, which was easily recognizable on account of its neatness, its peaceful atmosphere, and its two temples. The Shiva temple, as usual, was on his right as he entered, while that of Vishnu Perumal stood at the other end of the village, facing down the street.

Poor Vanya! All his fine assurance had already deserted him. However, he forced himself to walk slowly, very slowly, between the two rows of houses. There were indeed some open doors (one must never ask for *bhikshā* from a house where the door is shut), but he no longer had the courage to approach them. He hoped that he might at least meet someone who would recognize him, but the street was deserted. In fact, as he later remembered, in the south brahmins usually have their meal about ten o'clock in the morning, and this was therefore the time when they were resting.

Finally he reached the other end of the agraharam. He thought of stopping for a moment in the shade of the temple of Perumal, for the sun had become unbearable and the dust on the road was burning his feet most painfully. Unfortunately, even the mandapa of the temple was closed. Then he thought he could see in the distance a small stream, or at least a pond, and made his way there through a repulsively dirty collection of huts and yards. Another disappointment; there were no trees, and the water was dirty. There was nothing for it but to retrace his steps and repeat his walk through the village, this time in the opposite direction. By now he had decided to fast, and had thought of some excellent reasons for doing so! After all, the guru would be coming back in the afternoon; there would be a good supper and, in the mean time, there would be the fruit and sweets brought by the devotees to celebrate his return...

Vanya had just reached this point in his thoughts, when he heard himself being addressed in English by a man who was rapidly approaching him: 'Come with me; the priest of the temple is asking for you.'

Vanya followed him in silence for about fifty yards, while his guide led the way, intoning softly as he walked. They passed the last of the houses. He who was the guest of the village was being brought to the temple of Shiva. The gate was flung open and the priest appeared on the threshold. Without saying a word, he performed the customary ritual; he poured water from a copper vessel over Vanya's dust-covered feet, then caught a few drops of the water in his hand and brought it up to his eyes, and finally made the great namaskāram.

This was Vanya's introduction to the temple of Shiva. The priest did not ask of him either his name, or his caste, or his religion. The robe he wore was a sufficient sign that he was one of those who, while still in this world, have chosen to belong to God alone. In welcoming him, the Lord himself was being welcomed. The gift of food that is offered to him is offered to the Lord—or rather, the rice which the Lord has already given is given back to him. Indeed, it is offered in a far truer fashion than when offered in the liturgy that is celebrated each day before the stone 'signs' in the Temple. In fact, among Tamilian Shaivites the act of feeding the servants of God is called symbolically 'Maheshwar pūjā', a ritual offering (*pūjā*) to the Most High God (*Maha-Ishvara*).

So it is not only in Christian monasteries that people are encouraged to receive a guest as the Lord coming in person, and so to wash his feet and read before him the holy Scriptures... There are these strange similarities, defying space and time, among those who have discovered the mystery of the Presence in the depth of their spirit—another proof, if proof is necessary, that there is no place in all creation and no hidden corner in the human heart that is not touched by the Spirit.

In Vanya's reception the Scriptures also had their place. In fact, as soon as God's mendicant had been made to sit down, the man who had introduced him sat down facing him and continued his chanting. Venkatesha was one who constantly had the sacred words of the Veda on his lips, reciting them uninterruptedly, in the same way as other pious Hindus repeat the name of the Lord in a never-ending litany.

Then the priest, with some water drawn from the temple cistern, sprinkled the ground in front of his guest, and on it placed a banana leaf, which was again sprinkled, and beside it the silver cup which was kept for guests. Then Vanya in his turn sprinkled the leaf, making the sign of the OM. The priest's wife brought rice and sauces, and served the meal. She also poured a little water into Vanya's palm, with which he blessed the food, drawing a ritual circle round it; then what was left he swallowed.

After the meal they brought one of the carpets which were used to decorate the temple on feast days, and on it the Lord's messenger was invited to take his seat. In front of him was placed a box filled with holy ashes, in which stood some sticks of sweet-smelling incense. Soon a knot of people, men, women and children, had gathered round him. They wanted to have the darshana of this newly arrived sadhu, whose skin was fairer even than that of the brahmins. They only asked to be able to show their respect by making the great namaskāram, and to receive from his hands as prāsada at least a pinch of ash.

In a few words Vanya told them how he had come to the agraharam, trusting that their piety and charity would not fail to give him a handful of rice as alms. For it is Ishwara who offers bhikshā, and just as truly Ishwara who receives it. Has not Shiva often appeared in the form of a beggar, in order to test the sincerity of his faithful ones? By the hand of one devotee the Lord prepares and serves food, by the mouth of another he consumes it, and finally it is still he who is present in the food which we eat.

'I was sure that the Lord would do me some favour today,' said the priest's wife. 'This morning , as I awoke, I heard the *palli* (lizard) singing in the East. I even mentioned it to my husband. And see, you have come.'

Soon afterwards Kailāsanādar, the priest who had welcomed Vanya, showed him round the temple, assisted by his father, a venerable octogenarian. The temple of this agraharam was dedicated to Shiva, the Lord of Kailash, the holiest peak of the Himalayas, and the chief abode of the Ruler of the worlds. This same name was also born by the present incumbent of the temple. The mystery of the *Shakti*—the manifestation in the universe of the almighty power of God—was reverenced there under the name of Kāmachi Ammān. Vanya was shown the various shrines—that of Ganapati Vigneshwara, the 'Commander of the heavenly hosts' and the 'surmounter of obstacles'; that of Dakshinamūrti, the Silent Teacher, with his two hands held out, one in the gesture of grace, the other in that of wisdom; that of Murugan, the god of the most ancient Tamil tradition, later identified with Subramanian or Skanda or Shanmukha of the northern tradition; and finally, the central shrine, that of the Shivalinga. Behind the temple there was a minute garden, with a few trees, some flowers and a well for ritual purposes. In front of the temple was a mandapa, or pillared hall, built quite recently with the contributions of the village people. Vanya was also shown with pride the articles used for worship which had recently been brought from Kumbakonam by pilgrims to the Kumbha Mela.

When the sun was a little nearer to the horizon, the priest took Vanya to the river Pennar which was a few hundred yards away. The river bed was almost dry, apart from a small trickle of water half way across. From this Kailāsanādar wetted his hands and his face, and then reverently sipped a few drops. After that he drew from his girdle the small bag of ashes from which he was never parted, mixed a little of the ash with water, and with the paste traced the three symbolic white lines on his forehead and chest.

* * *

On their return to the village Vanya needed little persuasion to remain in the agraharam until the guru's arrival, which they assured him would at once be known.

It was now the time for evening worship. Vanya had often been present at the worship in big temples, but it had seldom made such an impression on him as it did that evening in the unpretentious temple of the village.

It is worth remembering that for the Hindu the two most sacred times of the day are just the same as they were for the most ancient Christian tradition—the mysterious moments of the *sandhyā*, the 'meeting' between the night (or day) which is ending, and the day (or night) which is beginning, the time immediately before or after sunrise and sunset.

With the first light of day the brahmin will be found standing in the river, awaiting the mystic hour. If there is no river near at hand, he will at least have placed a vessel of pure water beside him. Water is in fact the 'witness' of every act of worship, and can even take the place of the image, if one is not available. The brahmin then takes his bath, recites his mantras, especially the *gāyatrī*, and performs the ritual sprinkling of his head, forehead, ears, eyes, each sense organ and every part of his body, thus as it were consecrating them, and at the same time offering the element of water to the deities, *devas*, who are supposed to preside over the various functions of human life. He turns with folded hands towards the four points of the compass in reverence for the deities who guard them. He throws some water in the four principal directions around him, and then three times immerses himself in the water, having closed his nose and ears with his fingers. Finally, when the sun appears, he rises, places his hands together above his head and prostrates in the magnificent Hindu gesture of adoration towards the heavenly body, as it grows brighter and climbs into the sky.

Should such rites be labelled as idolatry? The thought will only occur to those whose souls are totally insensitive to the mystery—at once inward and cosmic—of the 'holy light', to that marvellous showing forth of God's glory in his creation—one which takes place in accordance with the very rhythm of time, or rather, which causes time itself to unfold and brings it into existence, in accordance with the rhythm of the infinite freedom of God. In fact, there is probably nowhere else in the world where the mystery of the Presence has been felt as intensely as it has been in India since the remotest Vedic times—and that as a supremely active presence, the whole sphere of the divine Shakti, which somewhat resembles the *shekinah* of Jewish tradition. It is a presence that is immanent in every being that has issued from the hands of the Creator, in every phase of the life of mankind and of the world, in the cycles of days, months and years, each of which depends on the phases of the heavenly bodies in which the spiritual and uncreated light shows itself in material form for the benefit of mankind.

The mystery of light is thus linked with that of water—water from which, according to the Vedas, fire is born; water which purifies and gives life; water which, in the symbolism of Genesis, was present at the origin of all living beings, and which Christianity was to honour as the sacrament of rebirth.

In India to take a bath is not simply a matter of hygiene, any more than it was at Qumran. For brahmins in particular it has the character of an act of worship. It is indeed questionable whether in a human life there are any acts that are totally profane; and the exacting ritual observed by brahmins is a continual reminder to the contrary. Taking a bath, as also every form of ablution, is in fact a life-giving contact with water regarded as the primordial matrix, and this is quite specially indicated at the vital moment of renewal which is marked by the reappearance of the sun. Moreover, among the brahmins of Tamilnādu there is no special word that means 'holy water' as such; for them all clean water is *tirtham*, that is, holy water.

The rite of welcome to the day has its counterpart in the evening rite of bidding farewell to the day, the liturgical entrance into the ambivalent mystery of night. Both rites stem from traditions handed down from age to age since those early times when rites celebrated on earth were regarded as essential factors in maintaining the stability of the cosmos and the regularity of the seasons. People in fact believed that through the sandhyā ritual the discontinuity between day and night and between the sleeping and waking states was resolved, and that it gave to time the quality of being continuous, alike at the human and the cosmic level.

The evening twilight is all the more favourable for prayer because, when the day's work is over, people can more easily put aside worldly cares and preoccupations and devote themselves without distraction to meditating on God in the Presence. It is above all at that moment that, in every part of India, the faithful throng the temples in order to worship.

In this agraharam there were about twenty-five or thirty households. Of the one or two hundred people who lived there, very few in fact failed to come every evening to the ' house of God' at least for a brief moment, in order to render homage to the Lord and entreat his protection.

The priest Kailāsanādar and his father were busy trimming the lamps in the various shrines and in the mandapa, and also carrying out the preliminary ceremonies of the puja by sprinkling water and offering flowers.

Meanwhile brahmin men and women were coming in and making the round of the temple, several times repeated, and honouring each mūrti (image) in the appropriate fashion—for example, dancing a few steps before Ganapati, meditating before Dakshinamūrti, clapping their hands as they approached the niche in which was Sindikeshwar ('You have to wake him up,' it is said, 'because he is always lost in contemplation!'). Lastly, when they came in front of the central shrine of the Shivalinga, everyone prostrated with their faces turned towards the north. Men and women, old and young, followed each other in this uninterrupted procession. The young people and the children—those handsome young Tamil brahmins, with their chests the colour of gold, their deeply serious eyes and their long raven locks—were not the least assiduous. It was easy to see from their faces and their movements how seriously they were performing the immemorial rites. The younger children were carried in the arms of their elders, and mothers would themselves place their little ones face down on the stone floor.

In the semi-darkness of the sanctuary the priests continued to recite their litanies, casting flower petals and leaves towards the sacred stone. From time to time the bell rang out under the low vaults, indicating some particularly important moment in the liturgy, when there was the offering of light in the āratī. At that moment the faithful would surge forward and crowd round the narrow door, so as to have the darshana of the sacred fire.

At the very end the celebrant came out, holding in his hand the dish on which the camphor was burning itself out—camphor which leaves no residue when it is burnt, a symbol of the soul which has vanished into the fire of the divine love. Everyone then came forward, touched the flame, touched his eyes and marked his forehead with sacred ash, in token of a deep need for communion.

The crowd departed and the outer doors of the temple were shut. However the lamps still flickered in the innermost sanctuary, for lamps which have once been lit to the glory of God must be left to burn until the oil is exhausted; there is no taking back of what has once been truly offered. Vanya took advantage of this moment to go all alone into the heart of the temple, to the small and mysterious central chamber where, equally alone, the sacred stone of the Shivalinga stood on its womb-like base.

5 Alone in the Temple

WHEN you enter the inner sanctuary, that of the Shivalinga, you can scarcely fail to be deeply impressed and to feel yourself carried off to the secret place of your heart. There is that bare dark chamber, separated by a long corridor, and sometimes by several ante-chambers from the mandapa where the faithful gather; and in the middle of it, the simple cylindrical stone with a rounded top which is intended to represent with the minimum of form the mystery of the Formless.

Outside the central shrine there are the various murtis. There is Shiva in the form of Ganapatu, the Commander *(pati)* of the hosts of heaven *(gana)*. There is Murugan, with his six faces, his peacock and his trident, who was born of Shiva, as also was Ganapati (or Ganesh) according to the puranic legends. Then there is Pārvatī, the mystery of the Shakti, under her different names and aspects, both kindly and terrible, the symbol of the share that created being has in the being of God and in divine fertility, both natural and spiritual; through her Shiva extends himself to the ultimate frontier of being. In the last mandapa is Natarājā (the King of the Dance), Shiva in his circle of fire dancing his dance of the cosmic *līlā* (sport), which is also a dance of victory, since he is trampling on the *asura* (demon) which he has just laid low. There is also Bhairava, Shiva in his terrible form as the destroyer of the worlds at the end of time. To the south (*dakshina* in Sanskrit) is Dakshinamūrti, the Master who teaches in silence, beyond words... All these are the various manifestations of the Lord, the recognition on man's side that nothing in creation eludes the divine presence and that everything in it is filled with grace and sacredness; indeed, every facet of nature, animal or human, male or female, has its gracious and also its awesome aspects.

The further anyone penetrates within the symbolical sanctuary of stone, the deeper he is taken into the sanctuary of his own being. There indeed, at the heart of his own mystery is revealed in the essential darkness the mystery of God himself, and at the same time, the ultimate and original mystery of all that is.

This is of course the mystery of God the Creator and of God who is Love, of God as he appears to us in his marvellous self-revelation in the cosmos and in his saving acts; but much more, beyond all that we can say, know or feel of God, beyond our own personal vision of God, beyond all 'recollection' even of ourselves, it is the very mystery of God in himself, of God in his true deity, his unoriginate being, his ineffable nature. This no word proceeding from the mind can tell, no sound capable of reaching the ear can express, no form visible to human eyes can reveal.

In the sphere of what can be heard, the sign of God's ineffability is the *pranava* (OM), the inarticulate vowel O(AU), the flattening of the primary vowel A—expressing at once the holy fear and the ecstatic joy prompted by entry into the mystery—which comes to an end in an indeterminate nasal after-sound. This is the OM, the final sound through which an attempt is made still to say something about God, once all the words and ideas conceived by the human mind have been discarded, before entering the definitive silence in which nothing more is said, apart from the eternal OM which no creature left to himself could ever hear.

In the sphere of what can be seen and touched, the Shivalinga is similarly the final sign of the One whom no form is capable of signifying, still less of embodying. The *linga* is at the same time 'with' and 'without form', as is taught by the Tamilian Shaivite catechisms. It stands at the boundary between the Manifested and Non-manifested, the last threshold that can be discerned through sight or touch by anyone who has sensed the presence of the essential Beyond, Parama Shiva—just as he was revealed in the appearance of the linga of fire on the summit of Arunāchala.

The chamber in which the Shivalinga stands is called in Sanskrit *mūlasthāna* or *garbhagriha*. *Mūla* means source or origin, *garbha* the maternal womb. *Sthāna* means place, dwelling; *griha* is house. So the shrine of the Shivalinga, we may truly say, at the level of symbol and cultic myth, is the supreme place of divine rebirth, or in terms of the Greek Mysteries, of the final initiation.

When the Hindu, following the path opened up by the ancient rishis, sets out to discover the inner world—beyond every sound, every form, every word and every thought, and also beyond the necessary experience and taste of death and nothingness—he finally comes at the last frontier of time to the moment of that total renewal which for Christians is signified and realized in the resurrection of the Lord on the other side of his passing through death and hell. Man's definitive meeting with God is birth beyond death. No one can see God without dying to self. No more can he attain to his own self in its supreme and final truth without dying, and therefore without being reborn—in the very realm of God. That is surely what in their own way the Shivalinga and the shrine in which it is hidden are intended to convey and symbolize. The dwelling place of God on earth—of which every temple is meant to be a symbol—must necessarily be the place of man's rebirth, a mystic womb from which he issues as it were for the second time, reborn in the very depth of the divine Love—now as a son, beloved and chosen from eternity, as the Christian would say, taught by the 'inward anointing' of the Spirit.

Europeans often sneer at the supposedly phallic character of the 'sacred linga'. The word *linga* does indeed have this sense, both in Tamil and in Sanskrit, but it is only one of many other meanings, all related to its fundamental sense as *sign*. Modern Shaivite writers generally object to this interpretation, and explain the crudely phallic forms of the linga which are found here and there as due to the degeneracy of certain sects. In any case we have no right to think that the Shivalinga, even if it was originally a phallic symbol, ever had the obscene connotation ascribed to it by those who disparage it—except of course in deviant examples. At all events, to its true worshippers it does not suggest anything indecent either in feeling or imagination. After all, the origin of life is essentially 'sacred'—however much it may have been profaned by mankind, especially in the so-called civilized world. Therefore, in a religious context, is there any reason why the sign of procreation should not also be that of rebirth, and besides that, a reminder to us of the high dignity of our flesh—which God not only created, but also assumed?

So Vanya remained for a long time, standing quietly all alone in the gloom, beside the symbol of stone. The darkness and silence of the evening made that inner chamber even more numinous. It was a powerful reminder of the 'cave' of the heart, the *guhā* which is so dear to the Indian mystical tradition, the true place (if it can rightly be called a 'place') of the unseen divine rebirth, of which the stone symbol is a sign and for which the symbol of worship is an appeal.

Under the influence of an almost magical enchantment, it seemed to Vanya as if he was being led continually a little further into his inner sanctum as each moment passed. Here everything seemed most wonderfully to express and release the archetypes that are hidden in the depth of the human heart. Indeed India's religious genius is such that, through its worship and the very structure of its temples, through its myths and equally through every aspect of human life, it constantly recalls you to what is essential, and ceaselessly invites you to discover in the depth of your being the ultimate mystery of your own self.

As the minutes passed, peacefully, happily, Vanya's mind was unable to grasp or think about what was going on in its hidden depths; he simply allowed himself to be carried along, letting everything go, only longing for that death which brings new birth.

* * *

All that night Vanya remained in the temple, alone—alone, but enveloped in the mystery of the presence. As Kailāsanādar had said to him, it may not be fitting for a worldly person to eat or sleep in the temple, Ishwara's abode; but on the other hand it is surely the true home of those who, while still living in the body, have already passed over from this world to God.

Stretched out between the pillars of the mandapa, throughout the night Vanya was at the same time sleeping and yet awake. What he afterwards remembered, what came to the surface of his mind, seemed to him to come from a very deep experience. Was it a dream? Was it conscious meditation? Who could say? He was as if possessed by an intense awareness of the Presence. Everything appeared to him as a *mūrti*, manifestation, aspect of God—all the forms which being assumes, and also all the forms, rites, hymns and sacred formulas by which mankind tries as it were to reach and tie down the mystery of the divine Presence, all were coming together and converging, in the Hindu myth, on the supreme symbol of the Shivalinga.

Everything on earth is indeed the sign, the linga of the Lord, of the One who fills all and yet is always infinitely beyond all. 'As in the first place I am myself!' thought Vanya. The hymns of the Veda, that is the Shivalinga; everything that is said, seen, thought or heard, is simply the sign of the One who is beyond all signs.

But is it possible to separate the Lord from what is his sign? No one will ever be able to make a clear and certain distinction within creation between what is God in himself and what is purely a manifestation of God. The least grain of sand contains in its very definition the eternity and self-originate nature of God. It would not exist, if God were not in the first place the Eternal and Unique One. The linga is a sign, and this is its very essence. There is no sign apart from the giver of the sign and that which is signified. There is no son, unless there is someone to have been his father. There is nothing material which does not proclaim the presence of spirit; it is in fact its sign, that which gradually prepares for its awakening and is thereafter its support, remaining inseparable from it. Shiva is everywhere present in his linga, wholly present in each point of the linga.

At the level of thought, nothing can divide Shiva from the linga in which he manifests himself. For this, *advaita*, non–duality, is the only appropriate word. Not monism, not dualism; but that sheer mystery in which man, without understanding it at all, rediscovers himself in the depth of the heart of God.

Shiva is wholly present in the Shivalinga, in the linga that stands in the temple, in the linga constituted by the universe, in the linga which every living creature is. He is there at its heart, he is its heart, but a 'heart' which is not one particular part of his linga, either spatially, dialectically or ontologically...a heart which is totally 'beyond', and at the same time and for that very reason most profoundly 'within', being at once absolutely transcendent and absolutely immanent.

When once you have reached the heart of the sign, you realize that everything is essentially an epiphany, a manifestation of the Lord. Thereafter what is important are not the differences and disparities between the manifold manifestations, but the quality common to all of them—and to each of them in a unique manner—of being a sign of God. This extends from yourself to every conscious being that ever has existed or will exist, from the atom or the smallest living creature to the galaxies. In everything now the heart has been discovered—the heart in which all is discovered, all is seen, all is known. There is nowhere anything but God in himself.

Only then can the taste of Being be appreciated. And thereafter that taste—that, and no other—is recognized in every being.

The Shivalinga is a symbol of God's having passed into his creation, and equally, of the creature's having passed, passed away, into God... The Shivalinga stands at the frontier between form and formlessness, *rūpa-arūpa,* between what is manifested and what can never be manifested.

God is at once the object of vision and the mystery of non-vision. But in reality, he is not attained either by our seeing or by our not seeing, either by our acting or by our ceasing to act. God is the beyond.

God is also the Infinitely Near—

> further than all,
> nearer than all,
> within all,
> outside all.

And everywhere God is Fullness and Infinity:

> Fullness here, Fullness there;
> from Fullness Fullness proceeds.
> Take Fullness from Fullness,
> Fullness ever remains. *(Isa Upanishad)*

It is precisely in the vision of this Fullness that anyone attains to it, and at the same time attains to his own self. This is the essential mystery of the world, of all that my senses experience, of all that my mind conceives—my own mystery, in that which in me is most inward and most personal, that which is unmanifested and cannot be manifested of myself and of all things, that which is beyond the reach of my awareness, and yet which is awareness itself at its very source.

What then does it mean—to go beyond the world of signs, the world of the linga, of the *linga* which however is entirely Shiva, and in which Shiva is all?

Beyond anyone's reflection upon his own thought and upon his consciousness in itself, there can be nothing else except the direct apprehension of the self in the self and by the self, passing from the Shivalinga to Shiva in his essential solitude, which at the same time is all-embracing fullness....

For one who has entered this solitude there is no more any 'without' or 'within', but only Being. For one who has crossed to the further shore, as said Buddha, the Awakened One, there is no more a shore that has been left behind or a shore that has been reached, no ford that has been crossed or raft that has made the crossing, or anyone who might have passed over... only the eternal mystery of Being, unattainable by what comes into being, and yet wholly present in what comes into being, in which it is manifested.

No one has understood the secret of the Shivalinga, so long as he has not entered into Shiva himself, who is the heart, the beyond and also the whole of the Shivalinga—indeed, into that same mystery which everyone bears in the depth of his being and which torments him so long as it cannot reveal its secret.

In the Shivalinga, Shiva is at the same time *a-sparsa and a-khanda*, at once 'not touchable', absolutely apart, and 'not divisible'.

He fills all, he is everywhere, yet everywhere he is *a-dvaita, a-khanda*, having no division or parts within himself, and not divided from anything whatever that reason tries to imagine as outside him.

At the same time he is *a-sparsa;* he touches nothing and nothing can touch him. He is entirely apart, totally incommunicable—and yet communicating himself totally.

Shiva is completely present in himself and completely present in his linga, his sign, his manifestation. He is not distinct from his sign, and yet remains sovereignly free—the mystery of creation, which resides in God, but in which God does not reside.

As for me, in my essential being I am completely apart and yet completely radiant, self-communicating. Everything in me exists in separateness, and yet everything in me is given, poured out—mind, senses and body—and through their means is extended to the cosmic boundaries of space and time...

The jnānī is one who has penetrated to the source of his being and has realized in the hidden centre of himself the mystery of God in his self-revelation. He alone in truth is in possession of himself and he alone can truly give himself; he alone can love completely. Nothing can ever give itself out, unless it is distinct, separate. God's transcendence is the very source of his immanence, 'transcendence' and 'immanence' being in the end only two human words which endeavour to indicate that the supreme is at once beyond and within, that Being is at the same time *rūpa* and *arūpa*, Form and Formless.

Vanya thought about the faithful whom he had watched that evening, as they prostrated before the sacred stone. It seemed to him that these faithful themselves constituted the Shivalinga, and perhaps with greater truth than the stone in the visible sanctuary. Who prostrates, and to whom does he prostrate?

If this body is allowed to die and this mind lets itself disappear, it is precisely in order that there may finally emerge, all alone, out of the original matrix now at last attained, the 'pure sign' which is symbolized by the stone standing at the centre of the 'place of rebirth' —with every joy surpassed, and all peace transcended, as long ago the Buddha taught. For, in order that the sacred linga may be revealed standing in the centre of the cave of the heart, it is necessary that all should have been given up and transcended,

> peace, the feeling of peace, and even the thought of peace,
> joy and the thought of joy and every feeling of joy,
> all thought and taste for what is within,
> the thought and the taste of being oneself, myself,
> and the thought of having renounced all thought,
> and the taste of having renounced every taste...

Then only the lotus springs up and blooms, its leaves in contact with the water, yet never wetted; and then the bees come to drink deeply of its nectar.

Vanya went on to think of all the devotees who had so often prostrated before him, including that very evening in the mandapa of the temple—as if the robe which he wore made himself the very sign, linga, of the mystery expressed both in the glorious linga of fire on the crest of Arunāchala and in the humble stone linga hidden in the sanctuary of this village temple:

Shiva prostrate before Shiva,
Shiva holding out his gracious hands to Shiva,
all the *līlā* of Shiva...
and equally the galaxies revolving about each other in infinite
space,
and the electrons which dance, disperse and reunite, at the heart
of the atom,
and the protons in the nucleus which split and explode,
and the people who blow up the earth by reuniting them—
all that, the līlā of Shiva and his linga—
and the fathers and the mothers and the children,
and all the different nations,
and man become one with woman, Shiva-Pārvatī...

He then dreamt that someone was asking his name, that he was refusing to tell it, that the other insisted, and that finally he said:

Who are you that ask my name?
Who am I, of whom you ask it?
What is the meaning of this request?
Is not everything the līlā of the Lord—
you and I, and all that we say?
the mystery of his appearing
in the very depth of the Self,
Shivalinga...
OM!

6 *The Shrine in the Jungle*

ABOUT five o'clock in the morning the siren sounded from Tirukoyilur. Vanya rose and went to the temple well, where he sluiced himself down with plenty of cold water. He had only just returned when Kailāsanādar arrived, opened the doors of the sanctuary and lit the oil lamps in readiness for the morning worship.

The priest came up to his guest, holding in one hand his box of ash, and with the other vigorously rubbing some of the ash on his forehead as he sang with deep feeling *'Tiru niru, tiru niru'*, 'The holy ashes, the holy ashes'.

Sitting down near Vanya, he still continued for a while to sing, and then told the story of the hymn. It had been composed well nigh fifteen hundred years ago by Tiru-gnāna-sambandar, one of the greatest saints and poets of Tamilnādu, during a pilgrimage to Madurai. In those days the kingdom was ruled by a Jain dynasty, and accordingly the king took care to persecute the devotees of Shiva unmercifully. One day the heir apparent fell ill and the doctors despaired of saving his life. The king then betook himself to the priests of his sect, but their mantras were as ineffective as the medicines of the doctors. In response to the entreaties of the queen, a secret devotee of Shiva, the king finally agreed to summon to the palace the saint who was the talk of the whole city. Gnānasambandar arrived, went straight to the sick child, and applied the holy ashes to his forehead and body, singing as he did so, *'tiru niru, tiru niru'*... Naturally the child recovered, the king was converted and expelled the Jains from his kingdom; and once again the cult of Shiva flourished in the land of Madurai as in times past.

Kailāsanādar then repeated at the top of his voice:

The holy ashes which restore life,
tiru niru,
the holy ashes which obtain salvation,
tiru niru;

what does he fear, whose forehead is marked with the white ash?
what demon would dare to attack him?
what foe could ever defeat him?
tiru niru, tiru niru....

He then began to chant the *tiru-pali-elucci*, the superb morning hymn of Mānikka Vāsagar. This is the special hymn sung by Tamil Shaivites at the moment when the created world awakes, looking forward to the rising of the sun. It is a fervent appeal to Shiva that he also may graciously arise in the midst of his temple and reveal his glory and grace in the hearts of those who love him.

At this point he told Vanya the story of this Mānikka Vāsagar, the proud official of another king of Madurai, some centuries later. One day, when he was on his way, dressed in splendid robes, to fulfil some mission for his lord, he happened to pass near the temple of Peruntурai. There, seated under a banyan tree, was a holy man preaching. The fine official got down from his palanquin and joined the crowd who were listening. Soon he could restrain himself no longer. With hands joined above his head, he made the pradakshina round the guru and fell at his feet, totally forgetful of his own rank and dignity—and equally of the commission entrusted to him by the king. There and then he discarded his jewels and silken garments, abandoned his palanquin and servants, and set off as a beggar, wandering from temple to temple, and everywhere singing the praises of Shiva, the God Beloved of mankind. This is just one example of the *līlā* of Shiva in the Tamil country, where he so often manifested himself—here as a beggar, there as a teacher of wisdom—to draw to himself the hearts of his chosen ones!

Kailāsanādar soon left his friend in order to perform the ceremonies of the *sandhyāvandana*—his bath at the well, the ritual sprinkling of his head and limbs, the recitation of the *gāyatrī*, the offering of adoration to the cardinal points of the compass, the application of sandal paste to his forehead, followed by the three lines traced in ash on the sixteen parts of the body. Then he went to the small mandapa immediately in front of the sanctuary and sat on the ground before a low table covered with various receptacles in which were water, clarified butter, flowers, grains of rice and other objects, not to mention the little bell and the oil lamps.

This was the *ātma-pūjā*, as he afterwards explained, the obligatory preparation for every offering of worship in the temple. In fact, if Vanya understood him rightly, it involves the veneration of God regarded as dwelling in the human body and manifesting himself more particularly in the five senses which make it possible to communicate with the outside world and the five 'breaths' which sustain life. The human body, through the breaths and the senses each in their different ways, is related to and corresponds with the five elements of which the universe is composed (earth, water, air, fire, and space), with the five cardinal points (that is, including the zenith), with the sun, the moon and the planets which move across the sky, and with the Vedic deities which preside over the various heavens. It is therefore an extraordinarily evocative cosmic rite which takes place in the ceremonies and the mantras of the *ātma-pūjā*, all focussed on the mystery of the ātman, which is the centre alike of man and of the Universe, as the rishi Sāndīlya sang in the Chāndogya Upanishad:

This same ātman which is within the heart
is greater than the sky and greater than the earth,
greater than all the worlds...
it contains all works, all desires,
all scents, and likewise all tastes;
it fills the entire universe,
this ātman at the centre of my heart,
it is Brahman itself.

Now what there is here, in this city of Brahman (the body), is a dwelling, a very small lotus flower. Within it there is a minute space. That which is within is what you should seek, that very thing is what you should want to know.

As vast as is the extent of external space, so vast is the extent of this space within the heart. Within it are the heaven and the earth, the sun and the moon, all that anyone possesses in this world and all that he does not possess, all desires. This is the ātman, this is the Self, free from all ills and sorrows, without hunger or thirst, untouched by age or death, whose sole desire is for the Real, the True.

> This ātman is within the heart. Serene and at peace, it rises up and leaves the body; attaining to the highest light, it appears in its own true form, the supreme Person *(uttama purusha)*, the Self, the Immortal, the Fearless. This is Brahman.
>
> *(Chandogya Upanishad)*

* * *

The morning pūjā in the temple of the Agaram was the responsibility of Kailāsanādar's father. He himself went out every morning, whatever the weather, to offer the pūjā in an old temple which was at least five kilometres distant from his village, reached by walking across fields and waste land. He would never take any food before leaving, nor would he wear sandals or take with him an umbrella or sunshade, no matter how great the heat of the summer sun or how heavy the rains during the monsoon.

The income of the temple was minute, only just sufficient to provide the rice for the daily offering and the oil needed for the lamps. The priest used to receive as his share part of the rice offered in worship—what was left over after the gods were fed—and, at least as a rule, twenty rupees as an honorarium. At that time however he had not been paid anything for over a year. It was claimed that the temple fields were not bringing in anything on account of the prolonged drought. Like Tobit's Anna, Kāmachī Ammāl, the priest's wife, did not appreciate her husband's unworldliness, and openly grumbled about it to Vanya.

Kailāsanādar interrupted her, saying: 'Do you think I have the right to abandon my duty for such a small matter? For the last ten years, day after day, I have gone to the temple of Bālasundareswar to offer the pujas. And now, just for a wretched question of money, should I give it up? It is true that we are poor, and have only just enough to feed ourselves and our children. Even so, by God's grace, we have never lacked the necessities of life. If I refuse to go there on account of those miserable twenty rupees, no worship will take place there any longer, no lights will be offered and no mantras chanted—and that in a place which has been acknowledged by our ancestors as a very special meeting-point between Heaven and ourselves. Is that a fitting way to thank God for his continual blessings?'

Thus it was that every morning in all weathers Kāilasanādar continued to offer the daily worship in the jungle temple. He would leave his home at dawn and rarely came back before eleven or twelve o'clock.

He had so warmly enthused over the site of the temple, and especially its solitude, that Vanya asked if he might accompany him there. They set off together, walking in silence one behind the other, along the narrow raised borders of the rice fields, crossing streams and making their way through thickets. The priest was quietly murmuring his mantras, now and then chanting the hymns of Mānikka Vāsagar or other saints. The further they went in the open country, the more impressive was the silence, It was a solitude such as Vañya had often dreamed of and, wonder of wonders, there on the horizon stóod the imposing silhouette of Arunāchala.

After skirting a big village on their right they finally reached the temple. The priest had not exaggerated in saying that its upkeep left much to be desired. The brahmins responsible for its management lived on the other side of the river. Their devotion fell far short of that shown by those who lived in the Agaram and their first concern was clearly for the things of this world. And so, though the enclosure wall built of huge stones was still intact, the other buildings, especially the outhouses, looked very delapidated.

In the middle of the courtyard stood the temple, consisting of a large mandapa and the sanctuary, and the corridor which linked them. Round the temple were the customary small shrines dedicated to Ganapati, Murugan, Dakshinamūrti and other deities. An old sacristan from the village was waiting for the priest. He had opened the doors, lit the lamps and prepared the wood for the fire. The priest drew water from the temple cistern and sprinkled himself with it, and then set about preparing the rice for the offering. Meanwhile Vanya went for a dip in the river nearby.

Then he came back to the temple. Here there was indeed nothing to interest the archaeologist, still less the lover of the gaudy. Nothing but the mystery of the dark sanctuary in which stood the bare stone symbolizing the Formless One. Vanya stood for a long time in the mandapa, watching his friend as he performed the pūjā, and letting himself be immersed in the Presence.

The place was indeed entirely fascinating—the lonely temple which spoke only of what is within, and spoke only to those who were capable of listening inwardly; the solitude of its surroundings where no sound broke the silence, either from the neighbouring village or from the one on the other side of the Turinjal river; the river itself, which never dried up and was flanked by the trees growing on its banks; the outward solitude, which symbolized and induced the interior solitude in one who had left himself behind and had at the centre of his transfigured consciousness only the Presence—the Presence of the One, the Alone, the infinitely Alone. Vanya was dreaming that one day it might be granted to him to come back to this temple and settle in some secret corner, while relying on the charity of the villagers for his daily food.

On the way home he shared his dream with his friend who, however, gave him little encouragement: 'People would be continually coming to bother you, either to ask for prasāda or else to have your darshana. As for the brahmins in this village, they are not exactly pious—just see the state in which they leave their temple! After a few days they would get tired of feeding you. If you thought of bringing provisions with you, you would only excite the greed of the rascals in the neighbourhood—it would be so easy for them to rob you of everything in this lonely spot.'

Kailāsanādar indeed felt himself more or less responsible for this foreign sadhu who was staying in *his* temple and was unhappy at the thought of his running into trouble at that place... However he did not succeed in convincing him, and they decided to refer the matter to the guru. If Swamiji gave his approval, then every obstacle would disappear as if by magic, as the priest himself acknowledged. However the time had not yet come.

Vanya remained until the following day the guest of the village and of its temple, the guest indeed of Shiva, the Lord of Kailash, who had graciously received the stranger into his own dwelling and had arranged for him to be cared for on his behalf by his faithful servants.

* * *

Thus it was that Vanya spent three wonderful days in this out of the way village, living among his brahmin brothers as one of themselves—one of them, and yet distinct from them by reason of his having been set apart, consecrated.

He had of course come across many brahmins in the course of his life. He had met them on every possible level of human relationship, ranging from business and social intercourse to deep contacts with friends at the spiritual level. He had also read much about them, but this time of sharing in their life at close quarters came as a revelation to him. It is one thing to meet someone on the road or in his office, where he always wears a mask, or even to be visited by him in your own hermitage; but it is quite another to get to know him in his own home, among his family and in his own village. This is especially true in those places which have preserved the best of the atmosphere and traditions of old time, as was the case in this agraharam.

When at home the Hindu throws off his mask, and you see the real man as he reveals himself naturally in his everyday behaviour, living through the countless details of his daily life before your eyes, from his bath and his meals to his prayer and his visits to the temple. There are no doubt degenerate Hindus—priests who regard their religious duties as no more than a means of earning their living, hypocrites who use religion as a cloak for dishonesty, superstitious and ego-centred people who only seek to make use of God. But, thank God, there are still many people living in our towns and villages, for whom pride in their racial heritage is coupled with a deep sense of their responsibility to God and their fellow men. Anyhow these few days at the agraharam, as well as the following fortnight at Sri Gnānānanda's ashram, gave Vanya the joy of realizing that God's gifts are never withdrawn. However great the number of those who in their weakness or their pride fall short of the destiny of their race, by God's mercy there always remains a remnant, who resolutely hold fast to his promises and wait upon the Spirit.

There is little more to tell about those three days, passed almost entirely in Kailāsanādar's temple, apart from the pilgrimage to the jungle shrine and the daily visit to the river. The villagers vied with each other in bringing Vanya his food. In the morning it so happened that milk was sent to him from three different homes. At midday people competed for the honour of providing his meal, and in the evening once again milk, fruit and sweets came to him from several families. People also came to sit in his presence, sometimes during the day, but more particularly after the evening worship. They asked few questions, as they knew he was not fond of talking, and besides they themselves preferred that. The monk has nothing to say about outward things, and as for spiritual matters, he teaches far more effectively through his life and by keeping his gaze steadily fixed on what is within.

Children also often came to make a prostration and to sit beside him. Sometimes they stopped on their way back from school, still dressed in their shorts with their shirt-tails hanging out behind. But soon they would return, this time released from their disguise, with an immaculately white cloth tied round their waist, their chests bare, or in the case of the older ones crossed diagonally with their brahmin thread, the white lines of ash standing out on foreheads and arms, and their long black hair falling loose over their shoulders. They would talk for a while to Vanya, telling him their names and the names of their friends, and describing their games and their lessons. Then Vanya would make them sit in the posture for meditation, the so-called lotus position, silent and motionless, with legs crossed and feet resting on their thighs, their hands open on their knees, thumb and index finger joined, and their backs as straight as ramrods. It was marvellous to see how long most of them were able to remain in this position without the slightest movement, without even moving their eyes.

Kailāsanādar's son was one of the most faithful. In fact he scarcely left Vanya except during school hours or meal times. His name was Shenmugan, the Tamil form of Shanmukha—one of the many names of Murugan or Subramaniyan, the god with six *(shan)* faces *(mukha)*, he who sees the whole universe at a glance, and transcends all directions and every point in space or time. The child had been given this name because he was born during a night that is specially consecrated to Murugan. He was now nine years old, and gave the impression that this temple was truly *his* place and that, like his father and grandfather, he would spend his life in the service of Shiva, the Lord of Kailash, as the guardian of his house and minister of his rites. You only had to see the devotion with which he made the pradakshina round the temple, venerating the various murtis, and prostrating before the standing stone of the Shivalinga. He confided to Vanya that he did not yet know by heart the mantras used in worship; but, on the other hand, he knew exactly how to offer the flowers and to rotate the lights in the ceremony of *āratī*. He had even had occasion to take his father's place when the latter had been prevented from performing the puja on account of some ceremonial impurity.

Vanya wondered how he could best help this child, so pure in heart, to grow in the love of God. It was too early to *speak* to him about God dwelling within him, so he simply encouraged him to sit still, to relax and concentrate his thoughts within. He was sure that, in the boy's open and expectant heart, the mystery would make itself known in its own way without the sound of words.

One evening the child was telling him about the *pey*. (These *pey*, among the Tamils, like the *bhūt* in North India, are somewhat like 'spirits' in western countries. That includes devils, of course, but it also includes 'discarnate spirits' and the fairies and goblins of European folklore as well.) On the previous day one of Shenmugan's friends had seen an enormous *pey* on the path leading from the main road to the village, and the child went on to say with an expressive gesture:

'*Bhayam*, Swāmi, *bhayam!*' 'How frightened I am, how frightened!'

'Frightened of what?' asked Vanya very gently.

'Of the *pey*, of course; if he sees me, he will beat me, he will carry me off, he will kill me.'

'Is the *pey* really so strong? Tell me, if your father was with you, would you still be frightened?'

'Certainly not, Swāmi.'

'Well then, don't you always have someone with you who loves you as his own child, I mean *Bhagavān*, the Lord who is hidden within your heart?'

'Yes. Swāmi, that's true.'

'And isn't *Bhagavān* much stronger than the demon?'

'Of course he is!'

'So how can you still be frightened of demons, if Bhagavān is with you?'

'You mean that I ought not to be afraid of demons?'

'Most certainly not!'

'That's fine, Swāmi; from now on I shan't be afraid!'

Even when the temple gate was shut, Shenmugan would often appear in the mandapa, as his house was directly connected with the temple. Sometimes in the evening, when he came in like this, Vanya would be meditating. In that case the child without more ado would make his *namaskāram* and sit down with legs crossed facing the swami, keeping silence like him. He would then gaze at him, or rather, caress him with his big deep eyes. Vanya, for his part, tried to see into the depth of those wonderful eyes and, behind them, into the sanctuary of that child's heart where so clearly the Lord was dwelling.

* * *

On the Wednesday afternoon news came that Sri Gnānānanda had returned. Vanya accepted a final snack and then took leave of his hosts.

He had barely set foot on the main road when a car that was coming towards him drew to a halt. It was Subramaniyan Ayyar who, after bringing the guru from Sittilingamadam, had come to look for Vanya. Very gently he reproached him for not having come to ask for hospitality at his house while awaiting Swamiji's return. 'I would have been so happy to entertain you,' he added. 'In fact, as soon as I got wind of your arrival, I sent someone to pick you up, but you had already disappeared.'

In the same way on the day before, when Vanya was coming back from the Turinjal, he had met Sundaram, the eldest son of Sriranganatha Ayyar, who had also invited him to their home in Tirukoyilur. But the Gospel precept holds good in every situation: 'Do not run about from house to house; in whatever home you are received, remain there as long as you are welcome, and accept with simplicity whatever they give you...' After all everything that happens is all the Lord's *līlā* and his grace.

7 Days of Grace

ON THIS occasion Vanya spent two unforgettable weeks with his guru. They were days of peace and fulfilment, one of those very few occasions in one's life that one would love to relive exactly as they happened, one of those very special moments when one was conscious of living at a spiritual depth in which the whole world of outward appearance has been left behind and one has come close to what is Real.

The daily timetable was simple and also very flexible. At dawn you took your bath beside the great well in the courtyard, or else in the river which passed about a kilometre away—though in the month of March it was dry, or almost so. About nine or ten o'clock there was the meal. At midday, a short siesta. All through the day devotees from nearby or visitors even from distant places were coming to have the darshana of the Master. On one of the Sundays that Vanya spent at Tapovanam there was an absolutely uninterrupted procession of visitors, devotees or seekers, from seven in the morning until eight at night, so that the guru could only manage to escape for ten minutes for his midday meal.

This meal was often a real feast. On those days it would have been offered by some disciples from the town or from the agraharam on the occasion of a family festival, or perhaps an anniversary, or else it was simply to give proof to the guru of the donor's fervent devotion and to obtain his grace in return; for gifts of food are very typical of Hindus and their socio–religious customs.

On such occasions the ablutions which preceded the meal were distinctly ceremonious. The Swāmi was asked to take his stand on a stone beside the door of the simple store-room which served as the dining-hall. The disciple then washed his feet, pressing them with loving hands and decorating them with sandalwood paste; next, with folded hands he would walk round the Swāmi and make his prostration. Vanya's monastic robe led more than once to his being included in these marks of devotion...

There were indeed many things that Vanya learnt during those days! And at the same time he had to keep constantly alert in order to avoid committing some blunder by not conforming with the rules of proper behaviour which are so strictly observed among the brahmins of Tamilnādu. Such a lapse on his part would have been all the less excusable, since he had the temerity to adopt the special garb of those in India who have renounced all.

For example, one morning Sri Gnānānanda had an English visitor who was served with a cup of coffee. This ignorant fellow drank it in the 'disgusting' manner of Europeans and North Indians by bringing the cup into contact with his lips. After that no one of high caste could even touch the cup, not even to wash it. On the other hand, there was a French lady, a teacher in a nearby college, who preferred not to drink anything during the whole day that she spent at the ashram; as she explained afterwards, this was because she was not yet sufficiently adept at drinking in the Tamilian way, and wished at all costs to avoid a breach of propriety.

One day we were all seated on the ground at the beginning of a meal with our banana leaves in front of us and were religiously performing the ritual of sprinkling water over them. Swāmi Gnānānanda suddenly raised his head and asked his guests: 'Do you know the meaning of what you are doing?' The brahmins who were present had to admit their ignorance, in spite of the fact that since their childhood they had performed the ritual two or three times a day and knew all the mantras by heart.

'You ought to know the meaning of what you are doing,' continued the guru; 'otherwise what is the use of performing ritual and reciting mantras? Now see; you begin by sprinkling the ground, then the leaf, and then taking a little water in the hollow of your right hand you trace a circle round the food which you are about to eat. All this symbolizes, or rather brings about—at least to the extent that you care about it and believe in it—the setting apart of this food which is to nourish your body. In our life there is in fact nothing that is profane. Nothing, no movement of our limbs, no activity of our senses, is untouched by the sacredness which we bear in ourselves and which surrounds us. Water is the great purifier. It cleanses our bodies from both material dirt and ritual impurity, thereby also symbolizing the inward washing which is no less necessary. Every religious act is preceded by a bath. Which of you would dare to go to the temple, or even sit down to take a meal, without having first fulfilled this obligation? When you return to your home, are you not bound to wash your feet before crossing the threshold?—another sign that nothing unclean should ever enter the sanctuary of your spirit, which indeed is further confirmed by the well known exception that no washing is required when you are returning from the temple or the river.

'The body is God's temple. It is to the Lord who dwells within us that we offer as in a sacrifice the food which will be burnt up in the fire of the five vital breaths, *prāna*. Do you not begin your meal with those first five mouthfuls which are regarded as an *agnihotra* to the ātman? Your food is something sacred, as is also the meal during which you eat it. That is why it should never be prepared by hands that are impure, and still less eaten with unclean hands. To partake of food prepared or offered by an impure person would be to share in his sin and to burden yourself in this world and the next with the consequences of his misdeed; to eat with unclean hands or an impure heart would verge on sacrilege. That is why, as soon as the food has been placed on your leaf and before you touch it, you draw as it were a mystic circle round it with the water in your hand, precisely in order to fence it off from everything profane or impure and to make it worthy of giving nourishment to your body. After that it is the turn of your stomach, which is appointed to receive and consume this food, to be symbolically purified by the drop of water which you swallow. Finally you touch the ground with your finger at the point where another drop of water has been let fall, as an acknowledgment that all material blessings which come from God are mediated to us through Mother Earth.'

Swāmi Gnānānanda was extremely hospitable and often drove those who prepared or gave the meal to desperation. It might happen that fifteen guests were expected; the Swāmi would then make all his visitors stay behind and enjoy the godsend, and twenty, thirty or forty extra newcomers would appear at the feast. One day Gnānānanda terrified everyone when he got angry and spoke with a harshness that was quite unlike him. The reason was that the cook, whose devotion was unbounded, but as a newcomer to the ashram was unfamiliar with its ways, had not managed despite every effort to satisfy all the guests. The guru refused to sit down and eat until everyone else had eaten, or at least pretended to have done so. Next day the cook came early in the morning to prostrate and then asked for how many people he should prepare the rice. 'For sixty,' was Gnānānanda's terse reply. But in fact, on that day when the time came for the meal, there were scarcely a dozen to take part.

In the evening rice was again cooked for the 'secular' guests. The guru and his monastic guests would eat some of the fruit or the sweetmeats which ladies from the Agaram or the town never failed to bring. Sadhus are in fact supposed to take only one full meal in the day.

In the afternoon the brahmins from the Agaram regularly used to come and chant their mantras, as Vanya had seen them do on his first visit. Kailāsanādar was one of the most faithful and, when there was no school, Shenmugan never failed to accompany him. At the end of the *Sūkta* and the Sanskrit litanies Kailāsanādar often chanted the Tamil hymns of Gnānasambandar or Mānikka Vāsagar. One evening he brought all the materials for a very special puja which he wanted to celebrate in the guru's holy presence. It was indeed always a joy to see him officiating and to hear him singing, for he threw his whole soul into it. Besides, his voice had a wonderful resonance and above all endowed his ritual movements with a beauty and fervour that were truly impressive.

* * *

Vanya had decided, in consultation with Swāmi Gnānānanda, that he would keep silence as far as possible during his stay at the ashram—except of course with the guru—in order to escape questions and unprofitable conversations. He naturally wanted to learn all he could from the master. In the darshana room more often than not he was seated right beside him. This position fell to him by right on account of his kavi robe, but even so as a rule he was happy just to listen. His best conversations with the Master took place when no one else was present, or else in the morning or evening when only the closest associates of the ashram were there.

When European visitors came, Vanya made it a principle to leave the honour and pleasure of acting as interpreter to one or other of the brāhmins who were present. Their translation was very often in fact a distinctly personal interpretation of what the guru had said, and in addition, was sometimes more than a little confused. The interpreter would take hold of the Master's words according to his own way of understanding, and would then restate the little that he had understood with a view to adapting it to what he imagined to be the religious mentality of a westerner—which in his opinion would be some kind of vague theosophy. Moreover the words and expressions which are traditionally used in Indian languages to convey the Vedantic experience have no exact equivalents elsewhere. So how could anyone cope with it, when for him both Christian and Hindu mystical experience were no more than sets of undigested ideas? When people spoke to Gnānānanda about this problem of translation, he always answered: 'How can you hope to impart wisdom and a real experience of God through the languages of Europe? These languages do not possess the *śabdabrahman*, that divine sound which, coming from within, gives to words their mystical significance. They are meant for dealing with *vijnāna*, the secular sciences, but are absolutely useless for discussing *jnāna*, wisdom, the highest knowledge.'

Nevertheless Vanya did sometimes have to translate for the Swāmi, when the usual interpreters were absent. On those occasions it seemed to some people that he was communicating the thought and teaching of the Master more truly than the others, and they asked him for the secret of this ability... In fact you have to hear the 'word' at a different spiritual level from that to which the rational mind is limited... At all events, one day when he was repeating to the Master in Tamil the question asked by some foreigner, Sri Gnānānanda merely asked him, 'What would your answer be?' So Vanya told him, probably quoting one of the Swāmi's favourite ślokas. 'Well then,' he replied, 'what are you waiting for? Give him the answer yourself!'

Another time a young Irishman called Peter turned up at the ashram. Like many others, he was touring India and visiting gurus in search of 'spiritual experiences', as they are called. He had been a waiter in a Dublin café when he heard the call of India. With scarcely a moment's delay he had left everything and set out for the Himalayas. Naturally he did not fail to visit any swami or ashram along his route, and this was how he came to Tirukoyilur. The pious women of Tapovanam devoted themselves to looking after Peter, cooking his rice and preparing tasty dishes with motherly concern. One evening after supper, Sri Gnānānanda told Vanya to ask Peter what was the object of his coming to India. 'To practise yoga,' said the young man. 'If you want to practice yoga,' replied the guru, 'then first ask yourself *who* wants to practise yoga; search for *that*, and forget about everything else, reading, conversations, travel, pilgrimages and so on. That is what yoga is!'

The teaching of Sri Gnānānanda was actually very like that of the Maharshi, but his approach and practice were different.

Sri Ramana never felt that he had any responsibility towards those who came to him. He never regarded anyone as his disciple in the strict sense of the word, nor did he ever call himself anyone's guru. People used to come to him, prostrate, tell him about their material, mental or spiritual worries, ask him questions, and in return they would receive at the most only a few words of encouragement. He hardly talked with anyone except those who lived at the ashram or were regular visitors. Furthermore, when he spoke, it was most often at a level where personal matters and the world of *māyā* played a very small part.

All that perfectly suited the pious colony which had attached itself to the real disciples and had settled in the shadow of the ashram. People came, morning and evening, most punctiliously, to have the darshana of *Bhagavān*—the women dressed in the best of taste, wearing their jewels and silk saris. During the darshana they would practice meditation and breathe in the mystic influence which was said to emanate from his person. Drawing-rooms resounded with lofty spiritual conversations and over cups of tea people discussed each other's spiritual progress. Sri Ramana was too shrewd not to be well aware of the snobbery with which he was surrounded, but he never said a word about it; he never gave orders, never interfered in the life of those who pressed around him.

Gnānānanda, for his part, did not hold with this kind of indifference. Naturally he never prevented people living in the world—people with responsibilities to family or society—from coming to see their guru, waiting on him, seeking his blessing, and so forth. Indeed, he even encouraged them and was not at all bothered when at times this was mixed with a trace of snobbery. In view of the spiritual level of such people and of the practical impossibility in their situation of doing more, he felt that they were doing well. However with anyone who was free from other obligations and spoke of devoting his life to seeking God and the things of the spirit, Gnānānanda was uncompromising. You cannot play with wisdom, you cannot play with God. You have no right to cheat when you claim to be committed to the way that leads to God. You do not hold forth on the subject of meditation, you devote yourself to it forthwith. Seeing that, as the would-be disciple admits, he has no urgent matters to deal with, he must give up running from place to place, talking about everything to all and sundry, reading every book that comes to hand. Let him settle in one particular place and devote himself exclusively to gazing within... There was just such a one among the regular visitors to the ashram in those days, to whom Vanya, on behalf of the guru, had to drive home these harsh truths and reminders of what is real.

One afternoon a group of people came over from Tiruvannāmalai. In the course of the conversation Gnānānanda inquired about various people, including some who had occasionally come to see him. In this way he asked for news of a certain English lady who had come to Sittilingamadam in the previous month. He was told that she was about to set off on her travels. Her itinerary was indeed extensive. It included the Philippines, Japan, Iraq, Holland, Canada, and several other countries. It took a little while for Gnānānanda to grasp what it was all about. But as soon as he got the point, his reply was scathing: 'What, at her age! What sort of a joke is this? She is over seventy. She has no family responsibilities. She has all she needs to live. She is not dependent on anyone and has no duty towards anyone. She comes to Tiruvannāmalai supposedly to meditate and to be solely occupied with her own soul. And now, lo and behold, she sets off to run round the world! What will she get out of it? You cannot trifle like this with wisdom or with God. If she is sincere and really seeking to progress spiritually, she should not stir from Arunāchala, she should give up all idle chatter and distractions, and should devote herself once for all to silence and meditation.'

These remarks were of course passed on to the lady in question that evening. She was just furious—'What right has that fellow to interfere? Anyone can see that he is not a jnānī like Bhagavān (Ramana). *He*

certainly never interfered in people's personal lives. He never judged or condemned anyone at all. That man was a real jnānī!'

8 The One Essential

FOR Sri Gnānānanda, *dhyāna*, meditation, was the one essential spiritual practice. For him it was the royal road, the only effective way of arriving at the realization of the Presence in one's own depths. One who truly wishes to attain to that has to sacrifice everything for silent meditation—depending naturally on how far he is free from family or social responsibilities. Having once provided for the elementary needs of the body, food, hygiene and sleep, he should only have a single goal and a single occupation—to practice meditation in the very depth of his being.

When Gnānānanda was pressed to explain in rather greater detail what he meant by *dhyāna*, he readily did so by means of short rhythmical verses in Tamil which he never tired of repeating and adding to.

Enter into yourself
to the place where there is nothing,
and take care that nothing enters there.
Penetrate within yourself
to the place where there is no more any thought,
and take care that no thought arises there!

There where there is nothing—
Fullness!
There where nothing is seen—
the Vision of Being!
There where nothing more appears—
behold, the Self!

That is *dhyāna* !

A young Tamilian arrived one day at Tapovanam. He had come from quite far off, and his plan was to find a room in the town, to come at set times to receive the guru's teaching and to apply himself to meditation under his direction. He explained his programme to the Swāmi, and added that he would take advantage of his free time to learn Sanskrit. Sri Gnānānanda at once interrupted him:

'There is no need for you to worry about finding a room or a hotel. You can perfectly well stay here and have your meals here. You will then be completely free to meditate as long as you like. As for learning Sanskrit, listen to me. They say there are fifteen hundred languages throughout the world. You will begin by learning Sanskrit, then you will want to learn Marathi, Bengali, then Chinese, and so on. Your mother-tongue is Tamil, isn't it? You must have read the Tirukkural. Well then, do not such and such verses (which he quoted) contain everything necessary for the spiritual life? And besides you also have in Tamil the Tevaram, the Tiruvāsagam, and so many other works left to us by the saints of days gone by. The Vedanta itself has been translated into Tamil. You have in your own language all that you need to teach you about the true knowledge. Why waste your time in learning a mass of useless things, when only one thing is really necessary? If you truly want to attain to *dhyāna*, far from trying to learn anything new whatever, what you need is just the opposite—that everything you may have learnt in the past should leave you and vanish, never to return.'

One day Vanya asked him whether a certain amount of *tapas*, austerity, was not essential, at least as providing support, for the authentic practice of dhyāna. 'Take your own life,' he said, 'your solitude, fasting and so forth while you were living in the mountains of Kashmir; and later on, your time as wanderer, going from one end of India to the other. And surely, at least for one who has taken sannyāsa, it is a duty to live in the poverty and total non-possession which tradition has attached to his calling?'

'Dhyāna alone matters,' replied Sri Gnānānanda. 'Everything else, whatever it may be—tapas, solitude, vigils, fasts, non-possession—is secondary, and has no direct connection with "realization". The only thing that counts is to free yourself from everything that prevents you from devoting yourself exclusively and completely to this silent interior meditation. Even sannyāsa itself is not essential. This ochre robe that we wear is much less for ourselves than for other people. The kavi colour acts as a direct witness and reminder to everyone that he who has taken it is one set apart, and that therefore they should not divert his attention with worldly talk, but rather assist him in every way in his life of solitude and close converse with God. A uniform is worn for others, not for oneself. The door keeper or the bus conductor would do their work just as well if they wore a white dhoti like everyone else. But their special dress shows everyone that they are the people to approach for certain things. It is the same with the dress of the sannyāsī to whom people come to ask for help in spiritual matters. As for the policemen's uniform, it serves to keep anyone who feels like committing a crime at a respectful distance and to make him stop and think. Does not the robe of a sādhu have something of the same effect?"

Another time, when a party had come to have his darshana, Sri Gnānānanda was repeating his favourite verse, 'There where there is nothing...' Some of the visitors started to comment on it in Tamil and English with varying degrees of pedantry. One of them proposed translating 'nothing' as 'void'. It was explained to Gnānānanda that 'void' in English corresponds to *śūnya* in sanskrit. 'But why, he asked, do you want at all costs to give a name to what, by its very definition, is devoid of all possibility of being named? As soon as you give a name to *not-being*, that which is not, you automatically make it into some thing. As soon as you give the place where there is nothing the name of "void", you are putting some thing there—and so you have to start all over again.'

Later on, when Vanya recalled this conversation, he admitted that he had never previously understood as he then did, the Buddha's teaching about the need for our meditation to be successively purified. We have to leave behind the place of thinking, then that of joy, then that of peace; next, in more advanced meditations, we have to leave behind in their turn all the negations which have acted as supports in leaving behind one stage after another, until we have passed beyond every affirmation and equally every negation, and have entered the total silence, in which one who has reached so far is no longer aware of being silent—since he has passed into the *ākāsha* of the heart, the 'super-space', which can no longer be circumscribed or localized.

Someone asked Sri Gnānānanda if breath-control, *prānāyāma*, is a useful practice. He agreed that it is, as do most people, but would not identify prānāyāma with the technical exercises for holding the breath. These are only useful as a preparation, by quietening and giving a rhythm to the bodily movements, and then, as a result of that, to the 'waves' of the mind. He took the view, as also did Ramana Maharshi, that breath-control consists above all in a very simple but steady attention to the breath itself, as it is drawn in and expelled.

He explained this by saying: 'The place from which breathing comes is in fact identical with the place from which thoughts come. The important thing is to hold yourself in this place which is the source of your being, and to keep careful watch to see that its silence and purity are never contaminated, and that you never allow yourself to be diverted or drawn away from it. Then when thoughts make their appearance—as they never cease to do—, in order to avoid being carried away by them, you only have to follow each one to its source, plunging into the very heart of the wave which is taking you to the shore, to find *who* is thinking this, for that is the fundamental thought at the source of all thought. In this way you come back to the place of your origin, the place in which all place has disappeared, the Self in which all self (ego) has vanished. Concentration on breathing helps towards interiorization. When you follow your breath as it returns to its source, you are also returning to your own source.

There where the I springs up,
springs up the breath
There where the Self springs up,
springs up the thought of self.
The place which is the source of the breath,
the same place is the source of the I.
At the very point where the self thinks itself,
the Self shines forth.'

Among that day's visitors there was a seeker after wisdom who had already 'done' a good number of ashrams and swamis. He was absolutely sincere, and also had an absolute faith in the teaching of his present guru. However when this guru insisted that he should make a final decision to devote himself at least for several years to meditation in silence and solitude, it was too much for him. Would it not be much simpler if the guru were to introduce him directly, as if by waving a magic wand, to that place of the heart of which he spoke so much, by using those marvellous powers (*siddhi*) which a guru must surely possess? After all, as an Indian example, there was the case of Vivekānanda to whom Rāmakrishna gave illumination in a single moment; and in his own tradition (he was originally a Christian) there was the case of Paul of Tarsus who was overmastered by grace at the gates of Damascus. —But of course with them it was a case of being already totally surrendered to God in the depth of their souls, so that they were not held back by pride or sloth; once the veil was removed which alone hid reality from their eyes, then with all the force of their being they sped towards the Real.

That disciple gradually brought the conversation round to the grace of *Isvara*, the Lord, and of his representative, the guru. Very readily Gnānānanda took him up:

'The guru appears when the place of the heart has been found. In order to reach it, personal effort and perseverance are needed. Underlying this effort there has to be one single intention which focusses all the strength of your being in a single direction. Singleness of intention, singleness of aim, the single-minded search for the ātman—this is the one essential condition of spiritual realization.

'You must have seen those young divers at the sea-ports who wait for passengers to throw down small coins from the deck. The ātman is like a coin which has fallen to the bottom of the sea. In order to recover it, you have to dive straight down, holding your breath, and with your body held straight as an arrow. The sea is the mind, *manas*. The waves are the *vritti*, the ceaseless movements of our mind, the eddies of our thoughts. To see where to dive, you have to still the waves.. To discover the place of the ātman, you have to still your thoughts. To still the waves you have to find what is causing them, to know where they are coming from. In the same way we have to seek within ourselves the place in which our thoughts are born and from which they fly out in all directions. When the water has become calm and clear, it is a simple matter to find the coin. And, he added with a smile, the mind can even become so calm and motionless that it is as if the water had been frozen solid!

'The grace of the guru, the grace of the Lord, is the seed sown in the ground. No one, whoever he be, is ever deprived of this seed. But is it enough simply to place the seed in the ground? Does not the soil have to be prepared, manured and watered? Otherwise, what is the use of sowing the seed? And once the seed has germinated, don't you have to continue watering, hoeing, pulling out the weeds? All that is the *effort*, which no one can shirk, and without which grace cannot do its work in you.

'Do you make a fire with green wood? You have to cut down the branch and let it dry. Only after that it will burn. So the fire is grace; the preparation of the wood is the *sādhana*, the effort made by one who really wants to succeed.

'You should have only one goal. You make inquiries about the goal, but once it is sighted, you don't waste your time in inquiring all over again. You go straight ahead in the direction that you have decided to go.

'What is the use of running about from master to master? What good does it do to spend your time reading and inquiring about different methods? Reading and making inquiries are like studying the map and the timetable. If you want to arrive at the place shown on the map and in the timetable, you have eventually to decide to take the train. It is the train that will take you to Madras or Bombay, not the timetable. A plan has to be put into operation, otherwise it is useless. When you go to the station or the market, do you ask the way from every passer-by? Do you stop at every signpost to find which way to go? If you do, you are likely to reach the station after the train has left, or the market after the shops are closed.

'Whoever truly desires something, desires it with his whole being and gives up everything in order to obtain it. You know the parable in the Vedanta: If your clothes catch fire and there is a pond nearby, you rush towards it without stopping to think, and plunge head first into the water. The same is true of anyone who really wants to discover the pearl hidden in the depth of his heart. He does not waste time talking about it.

'What is the use of feeling all the fruit on a tree? This one is too ripe, that one is not ripe enough. This teaching appeals to me, but there is one point in it that bothers me. That teaching does not have that drawback, but there is something else... Anyone who is really hungry does not take long to choose one of the mangoes on the tree and get his teeth into it.'

The disciple at whom this was aimed, reacted with: 'It sometimes happens that people who devote themselves to mental concentration go off their heads!'

'If my neighbour's child has died, is that a reason for me not to get married?' was Gnānānanda's pointed reply.

'I have a field. I need a well to irrigate it. I start digging one, and come to solid rock. Am I going to stop and fold my arms? If I want to eat, I need rice, and so a field in which to grow it, and so water with which to irrigate it. In one way or another I shall take no rest until I have found water.'

The disciple continued to argue: 'Could one not simply wait for "that" to happen? When you put fruit in the sun, it ripens on its own.'

The guru was quick to reply: 'There is still the need to put it in the sun. That precisely is your sādhana.'

Another time someone asked: 'What value is there in ritual and prayer—in hymns, or in the repetition of the divine name, *japa*? Are they necessary, or even useful, for attaining to spiritual realization?'

'Far from being useful or necessary, they are on the contrary obstacles for anyone who is following the way of *jnāna*. They should be firmly put aside. *Dhyāna* is the one thing necessary, and it is absolutely essential. Pūjā, japa, ritual, litanies and the rest, they all fall within the sphere of externals, they belong to the world of appearances and have nothing to do with the Real. To be attached to them and delight in them, to practice them assiduously with the idea that they are an effective way of coming to spiritual realization is a fundamental mistake, which will prevent the sādhaka from reaching his goal. Their only value is for beginners, for those who have not yet heard the call of what is within, for those who are married, who have responsibilities in the world and are incapable of persevering in meditation. Remember the biting irony of the Mundaka Upanishad on the subject of those who multiply prayers and sacrifices with the object of reaching "heaven". They no doubt do go there, but sooner or later they have to return to earth, so that finally they may find *brahman*, who has nothing to do with any heaven whatever.'

'But supposing I have to perform them,' went on the inquirer, 'for example, on account of my social or professional duties?'

'Then do so, simply and without being attached to them, as the Gita teaches. You are doing them for other people, not for yourself. For you, they are part of the world of *appearance*, but people ask you for them, and those who ask for them really need them because of their spiritual and material condition. Perform all the rites that they desire, offer all the pujas and chant all the mantras that will make them happy. But you yourself should not be personally involved; and in any case, that would surely be quite impossible for you. Is the magician taken in by his tricks? He well know that there is nothing in them and that all his turns are pure deception. And so, when you are with people who live at the level of appearance, you have to speak to them in their own language. Anyone who dreams that he is hungry has to eat in his dream, even if he went to bed with a full stomach. See how children play in the street; they build houses, buy, sell, cook, hold weddings. But once they enter the school, they forget all about their house, their business, their wedding. A picture is shown on a screen; does the screen afterwards retain any trace or memory of it? So it is with one who knows, when he has to act at the level of appearance and has to help, according to their capacity, those who are bound to that level and have not yet received the revelation of what is Real.

'Only dhyāna matters. When once the call of what is within, the call of the real, has made itself heard, every possible moment should be kept for the practice of meditation. Only when you are firmly established within is it safe for you to come back into daily contact with the world.'

Someone else raised another question: 'Should one fast or do without sleep?'

Gnanānanda once again replied that it did not matter in the least. 'In spiritual practice nothing has any value in itself. You simply have to see what in fact helps or hinders your meditation. Adjust your food and your sleep solely with that in view, though it is certainly true that the night hours are the best for contemplation.'

He was asked about the different kinds of *samādhi*. According to the Indian spiritual tradition, *samādhi* is the final stage of the practice of *dhyāna*—ecstasy which is enstasis, and enstasis which is ecstasy; for, at that level, there is no 'outer' (ek-stasis) which is not fulfilled and completed in what is 'inward', and no 'inward' (en-stasis) whose inwardness does not include the whole of being.

Gnānānanda explained that there are three kinds of samādhi:

'The first is *savikalpa samādhi*, in which there remains a certain awareness of oneself as distinct, some "memory" of oneself.

'The second is *nirvikalpa samādhi*. In this there no longer remains either outward or inward, either self or other. Nothing any more makes an impact on either the physical senses or the mind. You can longer think or feel. People can touch you, move you about, lift you up, but you remain totally unaware of it. It is fullness, it is bliss; fullness of joy, fullness and joy inseparably, encompassing everything; the bliss of brahman, the bliss of the Self, the bliss of the ātman; utterly pure bliss and joy, total bliss and joy—purnam, ānandam, pūrnānandam, brahmānandam, ātmanānandam, akhandānandam... ' You should have seen how the Swami mimed his words, beating time with his whole body, as his voice stressed each 'ānandam'!

'Even more exalted, however, is *sahaja samādhi*, when finally you have reached the original state, or rather original point of the self—original, because born-with-the-self (connate, *saha-ja*), or better still,"not-born", for in truth does being have an origin? Here you have passed beyond both enstasis and ecstasy. Differences are no longer perceived anywhere. The jnānī lives in the world like every one else; he eats, drinks, sleeps and walks about, just like everyone else. However, while others are primarily aware of the diversity of things, the jnānī sees them in their unity. In finding the Self, he finds himself and the self in everything. The *ego* has disappeared, which formerly came between "him", "himself", and other people, indeed, between his awareness of himself and his real being. Nothing henceforth obstructs the perception of reality in itself.'

The jnānī strides across the waters,
his head always high above the waves,
his gaze overpassing the horizon,
plunging into the limitless...
He traverses all that passes away,
his gaze fixed on what does not pass away;
in every thing he sees

that which is beyond all,
the end of all, the source of all,
the depth of all,
unique in all,
with no end and no beginning,
the eternal...
He has discovered himself and has discovered all,
beyond death
and beyond time in which at every moment we are dying...

'Bring me a fig, Śvetaketu.'

'Here you are, Swāmi.'

'Cut it in half; what do you see ?'

'The seeds, Swāmi.'

'Cut one of the seeds; what do you see?'

'Nothing at all, Swāmi.'

'So, my child, what you are unable even to see, from that very thing arises this great tree. Similarly, the Imperceptible, which is the life of all that exists, is the Self, the Real. You yourself are that, *tat tvam asi*, Śvetaketu.'

'Pour this salt into this jug of water.'

'It is done, Swami.'

'Now give me back that salt.'

'That is impossible, Swāmi; the salt has gone.'

'Drink some of the water; what does it taste of?'

'Salt, Swāmi.'

'Take some from the middle, then some from the bottom; what does it taste of?'

'It is still salt, Swāmi.'

'You see, child, you cannot find the salt in the water, yet it is there. Similarly you are not able to perceive Being, yet is here. This Imperceptible, which is the life of all that exists, this indeed is the Self, the real. You yourself are that, Śvetaketu.' (*Chandogya Upanishad* 6.12,13)

'That,O Gārgī,' said Yājnavalkya, 'the knowers of brahman call the

Imperishable, the Unchanging, *a-kshara*... It is the unseen seer, the unheard Hearer, the unthought Thinker. Apart from it, nothing sees, nothing hears or understands. By whom would the unique Thinker be thought? or the unique Seer be seen ?... This is the One who breathes in your breathing, this self of yours which is the Self of all things...'

(*Brihad-aranyaka Upanishad* 3.8)

'He who sees all things in the self
and has found himself in all things,
from what would he recoil?
He who has discovered Unity,
what sorrow, what illusion
can still touch him?
It moves, it does not move;
it is very close, and it is far away,
within all,
outside of all.
Thought itself can not catch up with it,
nor can any of the devas;
without moving, it runs faster than all.
Knowing and not-knowing,
both alike it has gone beyond;
having passed through death,
it has attained to immortality.' (*Isha Upanishad*)

The mathematics teacher who was mentioned above returned one Sunday. She confided to the guru that she had been disturbed by the spatial symbols which he often used.

'They are all,' he replied, 'simply pictures from which we cannot expect more than some temporary assistance, mere pointers or signposts. They have no value in themselves. When a child asks you where the moon is, you point it out with your finger or a stick. But where you are pointing is not the real place. So the *ākāsha* or space in your heart is an infinite space, which does not allow itself to be limited or localized in any way. So also in the sphere of the audible, you can begin with sounds or words which are uttered or heard, and from there go on to the OM which underlies every sound, and then pass from the audible OM to the OM which no ear, even the most spiritual, can perceive. The important thing is to have a starting-point, something which the mind can use as a support for its inward quest, a spring-board from which to launch out and pass beyond the superficial self. In addition it will help the mind to free itself from wandering thoughts. Breathing, a sound, a single point, awareness of the self made as pure as possible—all these are aids, but only for the time being, towards obtaining the vision of being.

'However you set about doing it, you have to settle yourself permanently within, even if finally the very idea of this "within" has itself to be abandoned; on that you should gaze, there you should enter and establish yourself, diving ever deeper until at last you disappear, as the Tamil lyric goes:

Thou who hast entered the depth of my heart,
enable me to give my whole attention
to this depth of my heart!

Thou who art my guest in the depth of my heart,
enable me to enter myself
into this depth of my heart !

Thou who makest thy home in the depth of my heart,
enable me to be seated in peace
in this depth of my heart!

Thou who alone dwellest in the depth of my heart,
enable me to plunge deep and lose myself
in this depth of my heart!

Thou who art all alone in the depth of my heart,
enable me to disappear in thee
in this depth of my heart!'

Sri Gnānānanda went on: 'If thoughts still make their appearance, they should be like the birds and other flying creatures which glide and move to and fro in the air; they should float in the *ākāsha*, the space of your heart, without settling on the solid ground where you take your stand.

'The essential thing, you see, is to make within yourself a solid, immovable dwelling place where no one can possibly enter, no one can find or disturb you. Let your "inner room" be closed to absolutely everyone. Keep it as strictly out of bounds as are our kitchens in Tamilnādu. As you know by experience, the place where the fire is lit and food is prepared is the most sacred, the most set apart, in the whole house. No one may set foot in it except members of the family or, in some cases, of the same caste. No stranger, even your dearest friend, is allowed to enter. He will take his meal on the verandah or in the courtyard. You should protect your heart from contact with anything that could defile it with the same care as you protect the family hearth.'

Vanya then took the opportunity to remind the guru of a verse in the Chandogya Upanishad which meant much to him:

> That which is at the centre of the space in my heart,
> it is the very same which is in the sun,
> which is in the earth,
> in the heart of every man,
> at the heart of every being.

'God is everywhere present indivisibly, *a-khanda*,' Sri Gnānānanda continued. 'The heart is the mirror in which he is seen. When he is seen in the universe, then his form is diversified, multiple—*bheda, dvaita*. When he is seen in the mirror of the heart, he is seen just as he is in himself, undivided, *a-khanda*, without any limitation or otherness, in the non-duality of being.

'Enter into yourself and contemplate, in the mirror of the heart.'

Here is a meditation which Gnānānanda gave to Vanya:

'The I is first of all perceived in its relationship to the world outside, to what is not-myself. So long as anyone only knows himself in this fashion, that is, by means of outward things and with reference to them, it cannot be said that he really knows himself. At that stage, what I call "myself" simply consists of the ceaseless reactions, sensory and mental, of that biological and psychological centre which I am, in response to external stimuli. It was on account of this instability that the Buddha would not attribute substantial existence to the person, which according to his terminology he identified with the ātman. Whoever wishes to know himself once for all and to arrive at his true being, should aim at reaching his "I" in its unchangeable identity and sovereign freedom. This "I" no doubt expresses itself in its acts of perception, both outward and inward, but it transcends all these and, in its inmost essence—the "imperceptible" of the Chandogya Upanishad—it is totally independent of them. It IS, just as truly in the absence of all perception as when its influence is extended and manifested through such activity—as is clearly proved by the experience of deep sleep, in which there is no longer the awareness of anything, and yet the person obviously continues to exist. To quote a saying of Krishna in the Bhagavad Gita, All things reside in me, but I myself reside in nothing.

'The "I" is not truly known, so long as it is not known in itself; no more can God be truly known, so long as he is not known in himself. Otherwise I would not exist apart from my relation to the universe, nor would God exist apart from the relation that the world has to him. This is indeed the metaphysical problem of the one and the many, of the same and the other, of the manifested and what cannot be manifested, which can never be reduced to any mental category whatever, for precisely, "who can think the Thinker?" Even reflex thought itself only apprehends the thinker and his thought in the form of an idea, and so indirectly. What is needed is to break through the shell of these successive abstractions and come to the central point, which refuses to be either localized or reduced to an idea.

'No one will ever reach his own self except through himself and in the very depth of himself, as the Gita says: *ātmani ātmānam ātmanā*, the self sees the self in the self through the self. No creature, whatever it may be, can ever do more than lead you to the door of the sanctuary, invite you to enter, and then bow and disappear. Nothing changeable can change into that which does not change. No inductive knowledge, not even purely reflex knowledge can attain to Being in its majesty.

> What is Full rests on nothing else;
> it is established in itself, on its own greatness;
> there nothing else can be seen or heard,
> there nothing else can be thought.

That alone is immortal,
that alone is free and unbounded in all the worlds.
Such is he who knows the *ātman*,
he who has realized himself. (*Chandogya Upanishad*, 7)

'There is no question that the most effective way of approach to what is within is to go by the "inward path". Even so the path vanishes, once the goal is reached. When you travel by the inward road, this "inwardness" is still an idea, and every idea implies duality and distinction. Its effect is inevitably to distance me from my goal, since it still distinguishes between the "I" which seeks and the "self" which is sought. So long as I distinguish within me the I which is within, I am not yet truly "within"... When at last that has been realized, then that which seeks and that which is sought vanish together—or, more precisely, what has vanished is the perception of them as different and separated. Nothing remains but *self*, being, pure *jyoti*, undivided and infinite light, essential light, the glory of Being, the inherent radiance of self, the vision in the self of Being in itself, the fullness of all joy, the bliss of the one who IS (the *Be-ing*).

'The final task in the spiritual quest is to resolve this ultimate distinction, that between the goal and the path, between the goal and him who is moving towards it. We have to overcome the dread which seizes the one who is in search of the self when he arrives at what seems to him, from his point of view, the last bend in the road. He then realizes that he must henceforth renounce finally and irrevocably everything in which until then it had seemed to him that he had his existence, his being, his idea of himself, and his self-awareness linked to that idea of himself. In the abyss of his heart, into which he feels himself irresistibly drawn, there is no longer anything anywhere to which he could cling and save himself from falling, no solid ground on which he could set his foot, no fresh air with which he could recover his breath. There is only the *ākāsha*, the infinite space in which there are no longer any distinguishable points of reference, which is not limited by any horizon, which is everywhere the same; it is no longer even an environment in which one could keep his place—rather, it has carried off into its boundless infinity and solitude the one who tried to keep his place in it... As the Upanishads often say, we have relentlessly to cut that "last knot of the heart", *hridaya-granthi*, that attachment which binds the Self to temporal and material conditioning and prevents it from attaining its nature as supremely free.' This was precisely the most characteristic teaching of Ramana Maharshi: It is the very thought of the I, of the I as distinct from the self, even if only provisionally accepted, that has to be relentlessly pursued, in order to make it flee from the light and finally disappear, just as a thief, when caught in the act, takes to his heels and runs away at top speed—as Gnānānanda, following Ramana, liked to repeat.

'This does not of course mean that we should pursue this idea with another idea—that would merely be to play the game of this specious and fleeting I. It is not a question of trying to persuade oneself that differences do not exist, that no one is ever bound by anything, that the ātman is the inner dimension of every being. All that is merely a matter of thought and imagination. When we take that line, it is like walking indefinitely round and round the mountain, instead of taking the steep path which alone will lead to the summit. The popular manuals of Vedānta often advise the sādhaka to think: "I am the eternal, the non-born, the non-dual, unlimited awareness, infinite bliss." But all that is quite beside the point; indeed, it is absolutely false at the level of awareness which the sādhaka has reached. Setting aside any idea of the "I", he should be reaching towards the intuition of the eternal, the non-born and the rest, and no idea will ever lead to this intuition. Reflection will never yield this truth, and yet only this truth gives salvation. The truth cannot come from outside or from within through mental effort. It quite simply springs up from the depth of one's being. It is the dawning of Light in the Glory of Being, arising in the heart.

'However that is only perceived as dawning in the moment of experiencing it; for, in the very experience of this dawn it becomes clear that there never was and never will be the dawning of Being, either in the Self or in beings. In the Self, as indeed in everything, at every point of space and at every point of time, and equally beyond space and beyond time, Being simply IS. The sun too only rises for those who go to meet it.

> The sun has reached its zenith,
> it will never again set or rise,
> all alone it stands at the centre of all...
> It has never set and never risen
> for him who knows...

Night is the same as day in the world of Brahman,
light unending...
Between this world and the other
the atman is the dam,
the bridge which leads to immortality,
but nothing from this world crosses over it,
neither death nor evil nor good nor sorrow,
nor anything that is transitory...

(*Chandogya Upanishad*,3.11;8.4)

'The direct method of realizing this is the practice of *dhyāna*, based on faith in the guru, in deeper and deeper silence of mind and the senses.

'I have to abandon the thought that it is "I" who experience the Self and has the darshana of the ātman.

'I have to abandon the thought that it is "I" who have the joy of seeing and possessing God.

'There is no longer a joy of his own for anyone who has come to the vision of being and who contemplates the inner light. For there is no more an "I" to enjoy and rejoice in—or equally to suffer from—anything whatever. There is only a single joy, the Joy of Being, the joy of Being in Itself, "God all in all" in himself.'

One day Gnānānanda summed all this up for Vanya in a verse of his own:

When I entered into Thy depth,
Oh! what happened to me?
Oh! what happened to Thee?

When I entered into Thy depth,
there remained no longer either Thou or I!

9 The Guru

ONE morning Vanya awoke about four o'clock and heard a conversation already going strong in the main hall. This meant that people were already speaking with Gnānānanda. He got up at once, so as not to miss the opportunity. However, as he strained his ears and tried to catch a few snatches of the conversation, he realized that the Swāmi's voice could rarely be heard. It did not take him long to recognize two brahmins from Kumbakonam, disciples of the Shankarāchārya of that place, who had arrived at Tapovanam the previous evening. On the pretext of conversing with the Swāmi they were simply showing off their Vedantic learning to their own great satisfaction. 'What is the use of going to hear those chatterboxes?' thought Vanya. He sat down again and meditated alone in his little room.

Two hours later, after his bath, he went up to Gnānānanda and made his morning namaskāram. The guru said to him: 'You did not join us this morning? It was splendid: all the philosophy one could desire—highbrow discussions on the ātman and brahman!'

Vanya replied, 'I was well aware of what was happening, and for that very reason, after thinking for a moment of coming to listen, I preferred to remain by myself and meditate in silence.'

'How wise of you!' said the Swāmi. 'All these discussions about wisdom and the so-called knowledge of brahman are just so much hot air. Dhyāna alone leads to the ātman which is brahman. All the rest is merely a childish game.'

There were certainly a good many aspects of Sri Gnānānanda's style of life which Vanya found hard to understand. His idea of the true jnānī was naturally derived from Ramana Maharshi, whose darshana he had once or twice during the last year of his life. In those days Ramana usually sat without moving on his couch, apparently indifferent to what was happening around him, enveloped in a kind of liturgical atmosphere. Gnānānanda, on the other hand, seemed incapable of remaining still. He concerned himself directly—too directly, in Vanya's opinion—with the construction work that was going on at that time in the ashram. He allowed people to chatter as much as they liked in his presence, and gave every sign of being interested in what they said. There were also plenty of other things which jarred on our European sadhu. Moreover, not all the visitors were as favourably impressed as he was. There were some who thought they could discern on the guru's face at least a trace of satisfaction when a car turned in and stopped at the gate, especially if someone with a white face got down from it. Others also criticized him for accepting without protest the various legends about his age, his past life, and so on.

Nevertheless, whatever may have been the thoughts at opportune or inopportune moments which passed through Vanya's head, even so when he came, morning and evening, to pay his respects to the Master, and above all when, alone with him, he listened to his words, he could not help feeling convinced that this man was truly the guru of whom he had for so long dreamed, the one who would enable him to clear the crest, if only he was ready to surrender himself to him with unquestioning faith. It was as if they were communicating with each other at a very deep level. The guru's words aroused echoes within him as no other man's words had ever done. It was as if, deep in Vanya's heart, profound secrets were then coming into view, secrets which seemed to be buried in hitherto undiscovered depths. What the guru said vibrated throughout his whole being and set off overtones which were quite wonderful.

In addition, Gnānānanda's whole personality radiated a wonderfully pure and tender love, a love which was totally given to each and yet was the same for all. So the joy of feeling oneself loved by him carried with it a high degree of detachment; for we all dream of being loved with a distinct and preferential love. But his love enveloped each one at the same time as if uniquely. You felt that for him all distinction, *bheda*, was annulled and had vanished. In each disciple it was as if he directly perceived his truest personality, the Self alone, the ātman.

All this will doubtless seem pure paradox to those who do not know the secret of the highest wisdom, *jnāna*, and even more to those—European and Indian alike—whose minds are cluttered up with ready-made ideas of which they are naively proud. No philosophy indeed will ever succeed in explaining or understanding the continued existence of personality at the very heart of the experience of non-duality or in the non-reflex awareness of being and the self. Indian jnānis themselves, being prisoners of their own mental categories, will often deny it theoretically in the expressions they use. However, their whole life, and especially the gift of their disinterested love, clearly shows that the personality—or whatever else it is called—has lost nothing essential in attaining to the absolute. Deeper than any awareness that he may have of it, the jnānī marvellously reflects in himself, as in a mirror that nothing any longer can dull, the very mystery of being, the mystery of *himself*, the mystery of God; and the Spirit, now given free play, realizes through him in the world the secret works known to him alone.

Many times Vanya questioned Gnānānanda about the role of the guru. But his replies always referred only to the definitive guru, the one who appears at the moment of the darshana of the ātman, of the guru who is the very light which shines from the ātman when it is finally discovered. 'The guru is *akhanda*, indivisible. He is *advaita*, non-dual. It is only this guru that can make you take the plunge; he appears and is manifested only at the moment when you do plunge. The other kind is the *guru-mūrti*, the guru in a visible form, the one who can only show the way.'

And that is why disciples never got what they wanted when they asked the guru for the kind of help that would spare them the need for personal effort. The self is only visible to the self, and the true guru is only 'yourself' within your own self.

Vanya one day asked Gnānānanda, to whom one could or should communicate this teaching on dhyāna.

'Certainly not to everyone,' the Swāmi replied. 'You have to start from the beginning: prayer, ritual worship, *japa* or continual repetition of the divine name—in a word, *bhakti*. You can only introduce people to the royal road of dhyāna when they are capable of it.'

'Yes indeed,' said Vanya: 'but my question is just this: Who are capable of it? What are the signs by which you can recognize those who should be invited to commit themselves to that path?'

'The shopkeeper must be able to recognize the things he is selling. If he cannot distinguish pepper corns from mustard seeds, or rice from millet, what is the use of his having a shop? Both salesman and customer would be bound to suffer. It is the same with the guru. He must be capable of discerning what is suitable for each disciple. If not, why does he meddle in such things?

'Now I am going to explain to you what a guru is,' he continued. 'Suppose you are following a road, going straight ahead beside a river. Suddenly you find yourself face to face with a sheer cliff. No way out. On either side the road is blocked. There is nothing for it but to start climbing. But the cliff is so steep that you are unable to do this. You try and try, but every time you fall back. Then you shout and call for help: *appa, amma, appa, amma,* Daddy, Mummy! just like children do. That is bhakti, the way of devotion, when you call upon the Lord who can do everything. Then, while you are crying out and bemoaning your fate, you suddenly realize that something has brushed past you. You look round. It is a rope, which has been let down to you from the top of the cliff. There is someone up above you, someone who has already reached the top. He is holding one end of the rope. He shouts down: "Hang on to it, hold tight !" He is the guru. All you have to do is take a good grip and, whatever happens, not let go—*śraddhā*, faith... But the guru must have sturdy arms and a strong back, or else the disciple's weight will drag him down, and both will come a cropper,' he added with a smile.

Vanya interrupted him, saying: 'But, Swamiji, you are always telling me that the guru only appears at the moment when the ātman has finally been discerned.'

'Yes, of course; that is the *jnāna-guru*, the *ātma-guru*, who then reveals everything. He says, Look, see!—and then all is seen, and there no longer remains either disciple or guru... only the one who deep down utters the *tat tvam asi*, Thou art That. The other guru of whom we are speaking is the *karana-guru*, the instrumental guru, in whom the real guru begins to take shape as the disciple becomes awake.'

Another time he said: 'God has four kinds of client. The first are those who from time to time wake up from their sleep, think about him for a moment, murmur "Lord, Lord", and in no time forget about him and fall asleep again.

'The second are genuinely pious. They visit temples, offer pujas, take part in pilgrimage after pilgrimage, sing hymns, practice japa, minister to sadhus—but it is all done with a view to obtaining material blessings, like health, wealth, or social position.

'The third kind are the true bhaktas. They do all that the second kind do, but they do it purely in the hope of obtaining spiritual blessings. Nothing else in this world is of interest to them. They only want God, and God alone.

'Finally there are those who no longer pray or ask God for anything—not even for God himself. They have no concern even for God himself. These are the jnanis.'

'But if that is so, Swāmi,' asked Vanya ,'then what difference is there between the *jnānī* and the *nāstika*, an atheist or materialist? He also has no desire or need for God.'

'There is none the less a difference, and an important one,' he replied. 'The difference is that the *jnāni* has no desire, either for God or for anything else at all, while the nāstika wants everything except God!

'There are the people who want everything except God, others who want everything and also God, others who want only God, and yet others who, having recognized themselves in God, are no longer capable of any desire, even for God.'

Those who no longer have any desire,
who are freed from all desire,
whose every desire has been fulfilled,
whose sole desire is for the Self;

those whose hearts have been set free
from all the desires which dwell there,
who have become immortal,
who have attained to brahman;

those in whom have been cut
all the knots of the heart here on earth!

(*Brihad-aranyaka-upanishad* 4.4.6,7; *Katha Up*.6.14,15)

The desires referred to here are by no means abstract or imaginary, but the very concrete and particular desires which at every moment beset the human heart: the desire for a caress or for a good meal, the desire to meet a friend or read a book, the desire to enjoy a marvellous 'heaven'...

Another of Vanya's questions was whether the jnānī is still has an awareness of his *sharīra*. The Indian word *sharīra* refers to everything in us which is not the ātman (at least as a preliminary definition, and to avoid falling into the western distinction between the material body and a spiritual mind). *Sharīra* includes both body and mind together, the mental faculties as well as the bodily senses. As for the Tamil word, here translated as 'awareness', its precise meaning is 'memory', 'recollection'.

'Yes, he does have that awareness,' replied Gnānānanda, 'but in the ātman, whereas other people have the *recollection* of themselves in their mind, their *manas*. In addition, the jnānī's recollection in the ātman is of all beings. In fact his sharīra is no longer peculiarly his own. Nothing belongs to him—but at the same time there is nothing that is not his.

'The same *prāna*, breath of life, permeates all beings, In the same way the ātman is everywhere, and everywhere it is uniquely itself. The jnānī breathes this "breath", inhaling and exhaling it in each created being. Nowhere is there any difference. Everything is felt by him as "his own".'

Vanya then raised the difficult question: 'Why does the jnānī always act well?'

No sooner had he asked the question than his mind clearly told him the answer. The reason is that in the jnānī all *ahamkāra*, all centering-on-oneself-in-isolation, all egotism, has disappeared. And egotism is truly the root of all sin.

However, the guru replied with the traditional paradox: 'For the jnānī there is no longer virtue or sin, good deeds or evil deeds. Sin, virtue, good, evil, are all matters which concern the *sharīra*, the *ahamkāra*, the consciousness of oneself-in-isolation. Differences and contradictions only appear to those who see duality. Whereas the jnānī is aware of things only in the non-duality of the ātman. So in an awareness like his, on what could the perception of good or of evil be based?'

In the course of the conversation Harold, who had returned that day, asked: 'Some people say that reincarnation takes place immediately after death. Others maintain that the discarnate soul has to remain in that condition for a hundred, five hundred, a thousand years, before assuming another body. What should we believe about this?'

This provoked an animated discussion on the subject of reincarnation. As soon as Vanya could get a word in, he admitted to the guru that to worry oneself about past or future births seemed to him a futile and indeed frivolous occupation. He personally saw no sense in the theory of reincarnation.

'I quite agree with you about not worrying,' replied Gnānānanda; 'but even so, how can one say that there is not a succession of births? There has to have been a cause for our present birth. What reason can there be apart from a previous life, which alone can explain both our return to this world and the particular circumstances of this return?'

'Very well,' said Vanya, 'but what was the cause of that previous birth?'

'The one before it, and so on successively.'

'That is all very well, but there must have been a first coming into this world. How can that be explained?'

'Who has ever been born?' Gnānānanda then replied. 'There never has been such a thing as birth and never will be—and it is the same with death. Hands, feet, eyes, breath, all these have a beginning, and everything that begins certainly comes to an end. But I myself? Even when the breath departs, does not the I remain?'

> The one who knows dies not, nor is he born,
> From where would he come? What would he become?—
> not-born, eternal, primordial, for ever himself!
>
> If the killer thinks that he kills,
> if the one who is slain thinks himself slain,
> nothing have they understood, either of them;
> no one kills, no one is slain. (*Katha Upanishad* 2)
>
> The immortal cannot become mortal,
> nor can the mortal become immortal.
> There is no decay, no growth,
> no bondage, no setting free,
> no prisoner, no candidate for release;
> such is the final truth! (Gaudapada, *Karikas*)

Questions and answers followed each other without a break between the Swāmi and his visitors. Vanya was listening somewhat absent-mindedly. His thoughts were on all that he had seen and heard in recent days, and the problems which this was bound to raise.

All of a sudden Sri Gnānānanda began looking intently at one of the visitors in the corner to his right near the door, and without any connection with what was being said at that moment, addressed him sternly: 'You are busy searching in every direction—this religion, that religion, this master, that master. Stop making such a mess of your life. Confine yourself to the teaching of our rishis in the Upanishads. To them truly Reality was revealed. It is all there. Useless to go elsewhere.'

One evening after supper Vanya sought out Gnānānanda in order to talk a little more freely with him. He was sitting on the big stone bench beside the well. Facing him, seated on the ground, was a young man who was speaking with great feeling. It seemed that he was talking about some people who had cheated him and had extorted money from him on the pretext of offering pujas, reciting mantras, and other such things. Sri Gnānānanda was trying to soothe the lad, but he repeatedly returned to the attack. This went on for a long time.

When he finally departed, Vanya went up to Gnānānanda, and this is what he said: 'Hinduism is a hotch-potch of superstitions and money-making. Everyone makes use of it to deceive his neighbour. Yet there is in the Hindu religion something that you can search for everywhere else in vain: the knowledge of brahman, the vision of the ātman, true wisdom!'

10 Festivals at the Ashram

THE following Thursday was *ekādasi*, the eleventh day of the lunar month. Tradition has made this a special day. On it many Hindus abstain from all solid food, or at least from their normal rice meal; it is also a day when more time should be given to prayer.

That afternoon, there was first the usual litany of the names of God, sung by the brahmins of the Agaram. But soon, from the Agaram and from Tirukoyilur, all the devotees of Sri Gnānānanda who were free, began pouring in; and from four until eight in the evening there was a marvellous *bhajan*.

The brahmins began by chanting the Taittiriya Upanishad in their deep voices to a very slow rhythm. The women then sang some Tamil hymns. Next Kailāsanādar struck up his favourite verses from Mānikka Vāsagar. Then Murugan Das felt that everyone should take part in the singing. He started singing himself, and at the end of each couplet or each invocation in the litany he encouraged the crowd to join in. With every repetition their fervour and devotion grew.

Some images of Shiva and Murugan had been placed on a stand in the pandal. Before them lamps filled with oil or clarified butter were burning, together with a large number of sweet-smelling incense sticks. Each new arrival brought flowers, fruit, incense, which was all heaped up in front of the images. Songs, scents, lights—it was impossible to resist the atmosphere. From time to time āratī was offered, a piece of burning camphor on a metal tray which was waved in front of the image.

A good many of the brahmins who had come for the bhajan on this *ekādasi* stayed at the ashram for the night. When they grew tired of singing and talking, they lay down just as they were under the pandal and went to sleep. Long after the others had fallen silent, Murugan Das continued singing hymns and litanies. Before long, as if echoing his invocations to Murugan, the sound of another voice broke the silence. Its rhythm and cadence strangely resembled those of Tamil Christian worship. Vanya was surprised and listened carefully.

It was in fact someone repeating an endless series of Our Fathers and Hail Marys, which alternated with his neighbour's invocations of Murugan. This went on for a long time. Gradually, however, the rhythm slowed down, the voices became weaker, and finally only single invocations could be heard at increasing intervals: *Yesuve* (Jesus)! *Andavare* (Lord)! *Muruga Tayare* (Mother)! *Mariyave* (Mary)!... then eventually all was enveloped in the silence of deep sleep.

Next morning Vanya went to the well with Murugan and the others for their obligatory morning bath. A peasant came up to help in drawing the water. He was particularly concerned at Vanya's inexperience, and with great devotion drew for him as many buckets as he could, which he then poured over him in abundance. Round his neck he was wearing a medal. Intrigued by this, Vanya asked him who he was. He turned out to be a poor villager who lived in a hamlet seven or eight kilometres away. The day before he had been working as a labourer at Tapovanam, carrying sand and bricks for the new buildings. As he had been tired that evening, and in any case would have to return the next day for his work, he had simply remained in the ashram to sleep. He admitted that he was the man who had been praying aloud so late in the night. It was his custom to do this every evening, he said, while waiting for sleep to come.

Vanya also met another Christian in the ashram. This was a local boy who was attending the high school in Tirukoyilur, and often came with his friends to visit the guru. Vanya had soon realized that this boy was different from the others. He did not prostrate, and even when he greeted anyone with the anjali, he had a way of doing it which showed that he was not a Hindu—there was something about the way in which he joined his hands and kept them close to his chest... The boy clearly wanted to meet Vanya, who for his part had no wish to talk to him any more than to anyone else. One day at noon, however, the student found his way to the small room where Vanya was resting. The latter made signs to show that he was not talking. But the boy insisted, and asked him at least to be willing to write down a few words in answer to his questions. Vanya made signs to ask him if he put Shiva's three lines of ash on his forehead. The boy crossed himself. Vanya then asked him his name. 'Gnānapragāsam,' was the answer.

'If you are a Christian, why do you come here? Don't you have priests in your village?'

'Yes, but I want to learn what Hinduism is. I want to read Hindu books. Please give me some.'

'I have absolutely nothing I can give you. Why not ask the guru?'

'I would not dare.'

'Then why come to me?'

'After him you are the one here in whom I have most faith.'

Vanya thought it best to close the conversation at that point, and once more, even more emphatically, referred the student to the priests in his parish.

Two days after ekadasi came the night of *Shivarātrī*, which was equally unforgettable. Every thirteenth night of the waning moon is consecrated to Shiva, but the one in the month of *māsi* in the Tamil calendar (*phālgun* in North India) which falls between mid-February and mid-March, is the holiest of all. People say that it celebrates the appearance of Shiva in the form of light on the summit of Arunāchala. The whole night has to be spent in pujas, singing and prayers, and on that night sleep is forbidden. On the previous day a strict fast is observed, to prepare body and soul for the celebration.

It was a repetition of the evening of *ekādasi,* but was even more impressive, and this time it lasted from eight in the evening until four in the morning. Precisely at midnight, a particularly auspicious and sacred moment, a huge oil lamp made of copper was brought in. Before placing it on the ground they sprinkled the earth with holy water, and a young brahmin woman drew on the ground the customary yantras. Then the lamp was lit, and round the symbol of light dances and songs in honour of Shiva, revealed in the glory of his light and grace, were performed without a moment's rest.

That night, among the guests at the ashram there was a brahmin from the town who often used to come and prostrate at the feet of Gnānānanda with his wife and elder son, Sundaram. On this occasion, however, his wife had not had the courage to accompany him. Her heart was too heavy and nothing could console her, because on that very night her second son Sanduru was to receive the solemn initiation into sannyāsa at the hands of Swāmi Sivānanda at Rishikesh beside the Ganges.

For several years Sanduru had been in close contact with Gnānānanda and had served him devotedly. At that time there had been two particularly fervent disciples, who were also very dear to the guru. The other was from Kumbakonam. Both of them were ready to leave the world for ever, if only the master would give them permission to do so. One of them he told to go and get married. The other, Sanduru, he advised to depart to the Himalayas, in order to free his heart more completely from family ties.

Sanduru had already been at Rishikesh for some months, and the moment had come for him to receive the kāvi robe, to signify his consecration for ever to a life of poverty, solitude and silent prayer. The night of Shivarātrī is often chosen for this ceremony. And so this was the night when he would have to renounce everything that until then had been his portion in this world, by symbolically throwing into the Ganges those things which marked him out as a brahmin—the cord of the twice-born and his tuft of hair—and by reciting for the last time the *gāyatrī*, the special mantra of a brahmin. His name, caste and family tree would be his no more. Instead he would receive a new name, given by the man who initiated him. The rishi with whom he would henceforth be linked would no longer be the one from whom he was descended by an uninterrupted series of human generations, but the one from whom he now traced his spiritual descent from guru to guru through the line of successive initiations. Furthermore he would have to recognize that the true source of his being lay uniquely within his own heart. Whoever indeed renounces the world before he has at least begotten one son to carry on the family line and ensure the performance of the rites due to the ancestors, is assumed to be doing so in response to an inner impulse so strong as to be irresistible. He has chosen henceforth to live without hearth or home, without any means of support other than the charity of the Lord's servants, and without recourse to those rites which for 'laymen' assure their relation to God. This can only be because he has already been engulfed in the abyss within and has experienced at least to some degree the scorching flame of the

Real, and therefore has no choice but to live outwardly also this all-consuming experience, now freed from every tie.

The thought of this youth whom everyone loved was very much present that evening. The master was delighted, and indeed a few days earlier had sent his blessing to this dearly loved disciple, as his spiritual father. All the devotees shared in his joy. The elder brother of the new sannyāsī also managed to do so without too much difficulty. But for the boy's father the sacrifice was heavy. He had dreamed of a bright future for his Sanduru; but now, would he ever see his child again? According to the strictest tradition, the sannyāsī is dead to his family, and his family is dead to him: Who is my mother? Who is my brother? Even so, Sri Ranganātha Ayyar received most graciously the congratulations of his friends, who were urging him to thank God for the grace bestowed on his family—for if to be born as a man, and above all as a brahmin, is already an incomparable blessing, how much greater still must be this 'sacrament' which, by cutting every bond, is the direct way of attaining *moksha*, the supreme liberation, the fulfilment and at the same time the end of all births? To Sanduru's father, Gnānānanda's gentle words and his blessing meant far more than all his friends' speeches of consolation or congratulation; but the poor mother had been unable to face the ordeal of coming that evening to prostrate before the man who had, as it were, robbed her of her child by revealing to him the royal road. She stayed at home, all alone, to weep...

The hearts of fathers and mothers are the same in every clime and every race. And likewise in every clime and every place the Lord's demand is identical. To those whom he wishes to call to himself, the Lord little by little teaches the language of the Spirit. Many and various may be the sounds which strike the ear and which God uses to make us listen, depending on the various circumstances of our human birth—whereas birth from God is unique. Springing from the depths God's call rises up irresistibly, and wherever it comes, it pierces the heart.

It was just at this time that Vanya met two sannyasis at Tapovanam who had received their monastic initiation at the famous ashram in Rishikesh. One of them was full of admiration for his guru; the other, however, spoke of him in a distinctly off-hand manner. But in any case the way in which the latter came to know Gnānānanda is well worth recording, as he told it to Vanya.

He had been living for some years at Rishikesh in the Anandakutir ashram, when one day—later, when Vanya told the story, he could not remember if the man had been awake or asleep at the time—he saw an elderly sannyāsī coming up to him and inviting him to come and join him. The sadhu's face was totally unknown to him, although he had travelled from one end of India to the other and in the course of his wanderings had come across countless sannyasis. The experience was repeated on at least two occasions, and Pūrnānanda became more and more puzzled. And then one day, quite by chance, he entered the cell of Sanduru, the young novice from Tirukoyilur, and was utterly astonished to recognize in a photo hanging on the wall the very same face which had appeared to him.

'Who is that?' he asked Sanduru with an emotion that can be well understood.

'Swāmi Gnānānanda, my revered master,' he at once replied.

Pūrnānanda naturally asked many other questions which were answered with predictable enthusiasm; and shortly afterwards himself came to Tapovanam in search of the guru who had such strange ways of summoning his disciples.

The other disciple of Swāmi Sivānanda was Swāmi Gāyatryānanda, who had recently been living in one of the temples of Tiruvannāmalai and giving lectures in different places on his master's teaching. He promoted the sale of Sivānanda's writings and, wherever possible, sought to organize spiritual circles like those which under the title of 'the Divine Life Society' are spreading the thought and experience of the Master of Anandakutir in many parts of India. This is why he thought of founding a branch at Tirukoyilur. He came to Tapovanam, explained his plan to the members of the ashram, received the guru's blessing, and set about organizing lectures at the temple of Vishnu Perumal. Vanya heard afterwards that he had not had much success; as his informant said, 'What is the use of all these societies and organizations? And, in particular, what is the point of seeking light and inspiration—that too through an intermediary—from a Swāmi who may be as holy as you like, but whom you do not know and who lives three thousand kilometres away, when all the time you have right beside you a guru who is worth all the sages in India?'

Nevertheless Gāyatryānanda was an excellent man and totally sincere. He unfortunately suffered from acute deafness, and could only carry on a conversation with the help of a rather complicated gadget, of which one end was handed to the person with whom he was talking, while he held the other to his ear. His patience was inexhaustible, and he used to make people repeat their remarks again and again until at last he had grasped what they wanted to say.

One day it happened that the Swāmi was due to return to Tiruvannāmalai, and Vanya had accompanied him on the way to the bus stop. They were conversing to the best of their ability by means of the ear-trumpet and tube. But this time it was Vanya who had difficulty in understanding. Gāyatryānanda was speaking about a certain swami whom Vanya simply could not identify. At times it seemed to him that he was referring to Sri Gnānānanda, but at others it was clear that it could not be him. 'Swami had said this, thought that, decided to do something or other...' In particular, he said that 'Swāmi' intended to build a hut close to Tapovanam, because 'Swami' was convinced that a given number of days spent in solitude and meditation would automatically lead to the darshana of the ātman... After that he spoke of 'Swami' having to leave immediately for Kerala. At this Vanya could not help interrupting:

'Do you mean that Swami Gnānānanda is going away to Kerala? No one has yet mentioned it. When will he leave?'

'Oh no, not Swāmi Gnānānanda,' he replied at once; 'I mean *this* Swami!' And the Swami's hand indicated himself.

Vanya had forgotten—or perhaps had not yet realized—that a true sannyāsī has lost his ego and is supposed to have merged with the supreme I—so how could he possibly speak of *himself* in the first person?

In order to safeguard the holy virtue of poverty, European nuns use—or used to use—the royal 'we' when speaking about their stockings or knitting-needles. Sadhus also have allowed their 'I' to float away downstream at the time of their initiation in the Ganges, and thus are reduced to speaking about themselves in the third person. But alas, *who* is it that is speaking about the 'Swami' in the third person?

Whatever might have been the doubts of Pūrnānanda and the unquestioning devotion of the other disciple, the following story which Vanya heard about Sivānanda in those days is well worth being told.

One evening in January, the coldest time of the year at the foot of the Himalayas, Sivānanda was sitting in meditation in one of the rooms of the ashram, surrounded by guests and disciples. Everyone was muffled up in blankets, their heads covered with thick woollen scarves. Suddenly a sharp sound broke the silence. Everyone opened their eyes and looked up. A long knife was lodged in the picture just behind the guru's head; it had first grazed his forehead, but had fortunately been deflected by his turban. People rushed forward to seize the culprit, who was led off to the police station. He was a young man from the South, whom like so many others Sivānanda had welcomed to the ashram with his unfailing kindness; he had continued to hope, against the advice of his close associates, that the poor fellow would eventually derive at least some benefit from the spiritual atmosphere of the ashram.

Next day Sivānanda came very early in the morning to the police station. He asked to see the youth. As soon as he saw him, he garlanded him and touched his feet—for beneath *every* form the Lord is present. He then entrusted him to the care of one of his disciples, who accompanied him to Delhi, put him on the train for Salem and provided for his needs on the journey.

* * *

On the following Monday the young brahmins of the Vedic school at the Sri Ramana Ashram were due to come to Tapovanam and pay their respects to Sri Gnānānanda. With a view to their visit the large pandal had been erected, while the guru's seat had been covered with a tiger skin and placed in front of the mats and carpets prepared for the visitors.

As the coach which was to bring the children was late, Vanya and the Swāmi walked up and down in the pandal, chatting together. At the other end of the pandal a group of two or three devotees were reading something with a conspiratorial air, frequently glancing in Gnānānanda's direction. He soon became aware of this, and asked them what was happening. At first they refused to tell him and tried to hide their paper. Gnānānanda however insisted, and they were soon obliged to show him what they were holding. It was a poem in Tamil, composed by one of them in the guru's honour.

'Please read it to me,' he said quietly.

This was too good an opportunity for Vanya to miss, and he sat down in a place which at the same time allowed him to follow the reading and to observe Gnānānanda's face and how he reacted. He listened to the reading with his usual careful attention, but his face never showed the slightest sign either of self-complacence or of boredom. Two or three times he interrupted, asked for something to be repeated so that he could understand it better, found fault with a construction, and finally suggested one or two grammatical corrections—and all with as much detachment as if it had been about a total stranger.

At last the children arrived. Sri Gnānānanda, ignoring the throne that had been prepared for him, sat down on the first vacant chair and then, with his customary kindliness and serenity, received each of the children. These came up to him one by one, prostrated and, once more on their feet, told him their names and family tree, meanwhile covering their ears with the palms of their hands.

Once the introductions were over, everyone sat down, and the young brahmins began to chant the Vedas, followed by Shankara's hymn to Dakshinamūrti. They then recited several *suktas* and concluded with Sri Ramana Maharshi's hymns in Tamil and Sanskrit.

When they had finished, Sri Gnānānanda asked their master if they understood the meaning of what they had just sung. 'Oh, no,' he replied, somewhat taken aback. The fact is that it is generally thought that to study the meaning of the texts would interfere with memorizing them. Before anything else, and without allowing anything to distract his attention, the Vedic pupil has to impress on his memory the words with their exact pronunciation, their rhythm and their intonation, precisely as these have been laid down and handed on by tradition. The study of their meaning can only come later, as the schoolmaster respectfully pointed out.

'That is of course quite correct as regards everything that concerns the Vedas,' replied Gnānānanda.' Everything about them is unalterable. They are not the work of man. They are self-produced, and no one has the right to change anything in them. They must first be learned; understanding will come later. However, do people pour water into a well? The water should well up in the well itself from some underground spring. It is like that with the hymns which we address to God. When you know and understand what it is that you are saying, then the prayer is welling up from your own depths. Otherwise it is like water poured in from one bucket and drawn out with another...'

* * *

Vanya only had two days left of his stay at Tapovanam. In one of his last conversations with Sri Gnānānanda he told him that he sometimes experienced that condition of which the Swami had several times spoken, which he called in Tamil a 'sleep without sleeping', and in English could be called 'waking sleep'. As regards the body it is a similar state to that of ordinary sleep; the same rhythm as in sleep has taken possession of the physical organism, but the consciousness remains amazingly lucid, a simple 'awareness', a simple state of 'being awake', but without any focal point to which this awareness is attached. If any thoughts or mental pictures do occur at this time, they appear and disappear as objects which have absolutely no connection with this deep and essential awareness, in fact rather like dreams.

'That is excellent,' replied the guru. 'But at that moment you still retain the idea of yourself. Now that is what at all costs must go. Always penetrate deeper and deeper within, until nothing more is left except pure awareness without any "memory" of yourself. Then the light will shine, the ātman will appear. The idea of yourself will be no more than a shadow. What is a shadow? Does it have a real existence? It is the same with all created things, the same with the world. In the light of the ātman, all that only appears as consisting of shadow.

'The ātman is within you the ground of all that your body does and perceives, of all that your mind thinks and understands. And you, who are the ātman, you are that which nothing can affect.

'It is in the ātman and not in the mind that you should be conscious of everything. In the ātman we should do our eating, drinking, walking, hearing, reading, writing; all should be done in the light of the atman. In all things the only reality is the ātman. All that exists derives its reality from the reality of this ātman. All that is seen is seen in its light. All that is heard is heard in the *pranava*, the OM, which is the name of the ātman.

'Not to know the ātman is the most serious of all illnesses. Ignorance of what is Real is a fever that is more dangerous for the spirit than malaria is for the body. But there is a remedy for this fever, one that is within the reach of everyone. It is available for everyone, I mean, *jnāna*, true knowledge, the knowledge of the self, the darshana, vision, of being. This medicine is provided by *dhyāna*, silent contemplation within.'

Vanya then said: 'If the cure is so simple, how is it that so few people make use of it?'

'Just see what children do,' replied Gnānānanda. 'When they are ill, their mothers prepare a suitable concoction and give it them to drink. But the children don't like the taste. They wave their arms, kick their legs in the air, turn their face away and refuse to open their mouth. If the mother manages somehow to get the spoon into their mouth, they just spit it all out. It is the same with ignorant people who reject wisdom.

'Wisdom, true knowledge, will never find entrance into anyone against his will. You have to want it, and to want it with your whole heart.

'Supposing one day you hear that on the other side of the river there is a swami whom everyone praises to the skies. So you want at all costs to have his darshana. You set off—but the river is in the way. There is no way to ford it, and swimming is too dangerous. Then beside the bank you see a ferryman with his boat. You ask him to take you across to the other side.

' "O.K.," he says. "But first, you must drop that bundle. I only take men, not their luggage."

' "Oh no, my bundle! I can't possibly leave it behind. How could I manage without my things? In it there is my food for the journey, my bedding for the night. I have brought flowers and fruit to offer to the Swāmi. I have got my holy books, which I read every day. After all, my bundle is not so heavy. Look here, ferryman, be reasonable! Take me across just as I am, with what I am carrying. I will pay the full fare."

'"Whichever you prefer," replies the ferryman. "The choice is yours. Without your bundle, I take you over; with your bundle you stay here. Which do you want?—the darshana of the Swāmi, or your old rubbish?"

'So then, when we have dropped our load, we pass over and have the darshana of the ātman.'

Tell me, who can run
with a load on his head?

What the guru expects of you
is yourself—
not what you bought,
as you went through the market!

Naked you were born;
only naked can you be reborn
in the glory of the ātman!

He who loses himself finds himself,
he who loses all finds all !
He who saves himself loses all,
and himself into the bargain!'

Finally Gnanananda repeated his favourite śloka:

'Where there is nothing,
there indeed is everything.
Enter into this secret
and yourself vanish from your own sight;
then only, in truth, YOU ARE!'

Glossary

a-dvaita	non-duality
agni-hotra	sacrifice to (or through) fire (*agni*)
agraharam	Brahmin village (or street)
ahamkāra	the sense of one's own I, ego; egotism, self-conceit
ākāsha	space, the most subtle of the five elements
a-khanda	not divided
a-kshara	that which does not pass away, imperishable
ānanda	joy, blessedness
anjali	a greeting with the palms brought together, either at chest level, or before the forehead, or above the head.
ārati	the ritual offering of light (a flame, either circled or waved before an image or a respected person)
Arunāchala	Sanskrit name of the mountain at Tiruvannamalai; *aruna* (the glowing colour of the rising sun), *a-cala* (not moving, so mountain)
a-sparsha	not touched
ātman	the 'self', inmost 'personality'; the principle of life undergirding everything
avatāra	descent, incarnation
bhagavān	Lord; also used when referring to specially venerated people, and regularly employed by the devotees of Sri Ramana Maharshi to refer to him.
bhajan	songs and hymns glorifying the Lord; also, prayer, meditation
bhakti	loving devotion; *bhakta*, devotee, worshipper
bheda	difference
bhikshā	religious alms
brahman	the supreme principle present in all things, the Absolute, the Deity
dakshina	the south; also, offering given to a priest or guru.
Dakshinamūrti	Shiva giving instruction in silence (his face turned towards the south)

darshana	sight, vision (see p.13)
deva	the powers who preside over the cosmic order (macrocosm and microcosm); personified manifestations of the divine power at work in the universe
dhoti	the garment normally worn by men, especially in the south, consisting of a long piece of cotton cloth wrapped round the waist and reaching to the ground.
dhyāna	meditation
dīkshā	ritual initiation
gāyatrī	a mantra taken from the Rig-Veda, which is the special prayer of brahmins
guhā	cave; used symbolically of the sanctuary of the heart
hrid, hridaya	the heart
īśvara	Lord; *Parameśvara*, the Supreme Lord; *Maheśvara*, the Great God
japa	murmured prayer; repetition of the divine name
jnāna	(in Tamil, *gnāna*; jna- or gna- is pronounced 'nya-,' as in 'barnyard'). *ātma-jnāna* is often translated as 'self-realization', 'realization of the Self/self'
jnānī	sage, one who is 'realized'
jyoti	light
karana	causing, effecting
kāvi	(Tamil) the ochre colour of the sannyāsī's dress
kshetra	holy place (originally, field)
līlā	play, sport; often used of the Lord's līlā, the free and unforeseen manifestations of his love and providence.
linga	sign, especially the cylindrical stone emblem of Shiva
mahārāj	literally, great king; title of respect
mandapa	porch, hall with roof supported on lines of stone columns
mantra	verse from the Vedas; set form of prayer; incantation
māyā	the indefinable state—in one sense 'illusory'—of the world of manifestation
moksha	salvation; final liberation which ends the cycle of rebirth
mudra	symbolic gesture with the hand
mūrti	form, image, manifestation; image in a temple
naivedyam	food ritually offered

nāstika	atheist, unbeliever, one who says "*na-asti*", "(God) is not"
nātha	(Tamil, *nadar*) lord
namaskāram	greeting, which can be full prostration
paramātman	the supreme Self, God
Perumal	(Tamil) title of Vishnu, the great (*peru*)*mal*.
pradakshina	circumambulation of a temple, shrine or holy person, keeping them always on the right (south), i.e., clockwise.
prakāsha	light, splendour
prāna	breath (Latin, *spiritus*; Greek, *pneuma*). *Prānāyāma*, control and retention of the breath
pranava	OM
prasāda	grace, favour; a portion of the ritual offering returned to the faithful; any gift from a 'holy man'
pūjā	ritual offering and adoration
pūrna	full; fullness (Greek, *pleroma*)
rūpa	form
sādhana	ascetic practices, spiritual exercises; *sādhaka*, one who is engaged in such exercises
samādhi	ecstasy; ultimate stage of Yogic meditation; also, the tomb of a saint
sandhyā	junction, meeting; the meeting points of day and night; *sandhyā-vandana*, rites to be performed at these times
sabda	sound; *śabda-brahman*, the 'brahman-sound', thought to be immanent in every meaningful sound, especially in every word that expresses spiritual realities
shakti	divine 'energy' (Greek, *energeia*), often personified in a feminine principle
shānti	peace
sharīra	the body, including all physical and mental faculties
shiva	good, auspicious; used substantivally as a divine name.
shraddhā	faith
siddhi	miraculous power
śloka	verse, couplet of a hymn
sūkta	Vedic hymn

tapas	**(originally) intense heat; fervour; commonly used for austerities**
vana	**(Tamil, *vanam*) forest, wood; adjective, *vanya***
Vedānta	**the 'end of the Vedas'; the Upanishads; the philosophy based on these texts**
Venkatarama	**Ramana Maharshi's name as a child**
vidyā	**knowledge or wisdom**
yantra	**sacred design**

Note

In this book Abhishiktananda described his meetings with Srī Gnānānanda at Tirukoilur, first in December 1955, and then during a longer stay of two-three weeks in February-March 1956. A first account of these experiences was written shortly afterwards, while they were still fresh in his mind, and to them were appended his recollections of Srī Ramana Maharshi and Arunachala. At this stage he realized that there was no possibility of such a book being published. But in the early 60s friends who had seen the manuscript encouraged him to prepare it for publication. He hesitated, because he felt he must preserve his anonymity and also because he was uncertain how to make the book acceptable to Christian readers. In the two versions which he made between 1961 and 1963, he adopted a pseudonym "Aruneya" and added an edifying preface and epilogue, a device which failed to satisfy him. Finally in 1968 he wrote the present version of "Gnānānanda" under the pseudonym of "Vanya" ("forest-dweller") and without artificial additions. When it was published in 1970, he said in a letter: "It is different from the other books, and presents the best of Indian experience without making comparisons or value-judgments." This is borne out by the welcome given by the Sri Gnānānanda Thapovanam to the English version when it appeared in 1974. In their own *Sadguru Gnānānanda* (1979) they quoted extensively from Abhishiktananda, and paid a handsome tribute to his work.